POINT OF CONTACT

CONTENTS

To Our Readers

This issue of *Point of Contact*, has been made possible in part by a grant from The College of Arts and Sciences at Syracuse University.

Our thanks to Kenneth A. Shaw, Chancellor of Syracuse University, Deborah Freund, Provost and Vice Chancellor for Academic Affairs, Cathryn Newton, Dean of The College of Arts and Sciences, Carole B. Brzozowski, Dean of The College of Visual and Performing Arts, Nirelle J. Galson, Director of The Division of International Programs Abroad, and Bennie R. Ware, Vice President of Research and Computing. Our special thanks to Robert Jensen, former Dean of The College of Arts and Sciences at Syracuse University.

We dedicate this issue to
John Cage and Nancy Graves

THE POWER OF SILENCE

Raimon Panikkar

Translated from German by Gerd K. Schneider

With the following fundamental reflection about the nature and power of silence, I do not want to mediate thoughts, only life, as I dare to approach silence with words. Words, if they are genuine, should be the revelation of silence.

From a christian point of view it is perhaps appropriate to remember this warning from the gospel of Matthew: "But I say unto you, That every idle word that Men shall speak, they shall give account thereof in the day of judgment. For by thy words thou shall be justified, and by thy words thou shalt be condemned" (Mt 12: 36-37).

SILENCE SAYS NOTHING

Silence says nothing. And it says nothing because it has nothing to say. Otherwise it would say something.

To say nothing, in order to keep something back from another person, is an artificial silence, a keeping silent, but not silence.

Birds do not speak our human language because they do not have anything to say. Everything they have to "say" they sing, and they make themselves understood in their manner.

Silence says nothing. Perhaps because it is the nothing which "says" silence. I mean that the nothing is silent. And the nothing can only be perceived in silence. And in our time, when we are bombarded with words, it may be appropriate to keep silent about silence, in order to become aware of silence and to become conscious also of the power of silence.

Silence says nothing. It says nothing that we can express by speaking in language itself. If silence had anything to say that could also be said in my speech or in the speech of someone else, then the speech of silence would be a contradiction because silence would cease to be silence.

Silence says nothing. Silence is inexpressible through words. And still we know that the inexpressible exists because the inexpressible is perceptible. Silence reveals itself.

THE MYSTERY OF THE INEXPRESSIBLE

When I state the existence of the inexpressible, then the inexpressible seems also to be expressible. However, what have I then said? I have only said catachrestically that the inexpressible does exist. About the inexpressible itself I have not said anything, because I have not penetrated the mystery of the inexpressible. My words were only signs which trace a superficial form. My words did not have any depth. But words, if they are genuine, not only trace or imitate; they are rooted in the depth of life and open for us a revelation of the inexpressible. Genuine words are mediators, mediators between silence and sense.

A word which fails to bring about and create this mediation between silence and meaning is a lie, and then it is that word which condemns us. Such a useless word is meaningless and does not effect anything because it does not bear witness to this realm of reality between silence and meaning which mediates silence and centers Man.

There, where this mediating word is missing, we do not find meaning. And vice versa, where there is no meaning, there is also no real word.

In false words the inexpressible is not present. But where it is present, it manifests itself as the highest jewel of language and we are conscious of the inexpressible.

The inexpressible of which we are conscious is that which language itself does not say but only hints at or maybe hides. The inexpressible only resonates in the spoken word and is only perceived by the listener. But not every listener can hear it; only the attentive listener and the loving listener will hear the silence of the word and perceive and understand something more in the word than only the content of the word. He will also perceive the sound of the word.

If we do not perceive the sound of the word, then we hear only a part of the word. A word without sound, a word that only says what can be recorded by a machine, is not a word. The word is more than a sound wave and the word is more than meaning. In the sound of the word we find our way to the core of life and we become aware that the inexpressible exists although it is inexpressible. According to Plotinos, the logos—the word—of the soul is a silent logos. The word of the spirit, the word of Man is a silent word. And precisely listening for that which the word pours out is part of the participation in the word.

To Perceive the Voice of Silence

We can perceive the inexpressible because our awareness is not limited to perception through our senses and understanding through reasoning. But awareness begins with perception through the senses. I see, I hear, I feel, I smell, I taste and still I don't quite understand what I perceive there although my reasoning power tries to understand all this. And although our faculty of reason understands much, the action and capabilities of our senses themselves are a mystery closed to reason and its understanding. I don't know why I see or hear, taste, smell or taste. But I know that I perceive something and that I am aware of it. And I can experience that my perceptive faculty goes beyond these two fields of awareness, that there exists something beyond perception through the senses and understanding through reasoning that the ancients of East and West have called the third eye or the third ear. It is an awareness which somehow is aware just of that which cannot be perceived and understood. It is the awareness of the inexpressible and of the unspoken which resonates and co-vibrates alongside the word and the content of the word. And we hear it if we are listeners, if we are lovers, because there is no real awareness without love.

The attentive loving awareness can also be called the mystical. The mystical in the sense of the direct awareness of reality.

The immediate awareness is the immediate experience of the wholeness, the All in the concrete—in a beloved person, in a flower or the sound of a bell. I will not become aware of reality through thoughts or concepts like universe, God or wholeness. The experience of life, the experience of the whole reality cracks open in the immediate encounter with the concrete. And still more: he who does not see a whole forest in one tree will not see either forest or tree. He who does not see and experience the entire mystery of womanhood, of manliness, of the human, or of friendship, in his or her beloved, in one's children or friends will never experience what it means to be human, to be a woman, a man, a child or a friend. And whoever reduces human life to that which he hears or understands lives a miserable human life which forces man to fight his way through life. This person has no joy, does not experience the fullness of life. At the end he has not lived a real life because life consists of more than to multiply these small superficial experiences which develop from contact with reality and to remain standing in this fragmentation of life. Life is rooted in the immediate encounter with the concrete.

The mystical is this fundamental awareness which lets me experience totality in a single object.

If we are capable of perceiving and experiencing totality in the concrete, then life begins to unfold for us. It is this experience which lets us witness that there is a connection between that which is said and that which is unsaid, between the inexpressible and the expressible, between the formed and the unformed. This connection is neither a dualistic connection—here the something I say and there the something else I keep silent—nor is it a monistic mixture of two things. This connection is Non-Dual-Advaita. We have to distinguish, we cannot separate.

The Impotence [Ohn*macht*] of Silence

What is the power of silence? The power of silence is its helplessness. Silence as silence has no power. Genuine silence is impotent (*macht*loss). False silence is threatening because it keeps silent what should be said. This threat originates because the listener suspects and maybe feels that which the silent person withholds and does not say. This keeping silent gives rise to thoughts in the listener and phantasies take form, so that the listener turns to these thoughts and phantasies and thus falls into fear and anxiety because he is not capable of hearing life. Keeping silent produces anxiety and suffocates life. Keeping silent something which was to be said and which the person in question does not dare to say is no silence.

Genuine silence is impotent. When I ask, and the answer is silence, then I am not allowed to interpret this silence as either yes or no. This silence leaves me free to do something or not to do something. The decision becomes my responsibility, and I cannot transfer or put the burden on the silent person.

When Jesus was asked what the truth is, he remained silent and left it to us to find truth in the right hand or the left hand, above or below. He did not want to bind us. He did not exert any power on the listening questioner because this silence has no power. To play a game of power with silence is insincere. And it is not only insincere, it will take revenge. Every word, even every withheld word, returns to the person who says it or withholds it because the listener and the speaker/silent keeper are a unity. Again we distinguish—listener and speaker/silent keeper—and still we cannot separate them.

Silence has no power, it does not threaten and does not command, maybe because it expects everything, because it is ready for everything.

The Listening Word

The power of silence is not silence. Silence is the silent testimony of trust. The power of silence lies in the listening word. Silence has transferred its power to the listening word and it trusts it.

The power of silence becomes obvious when the listening word transmits the silence and puts it into words, if it translates the silence into words. And every word which has this transmission and this translation has an enormous power. The entire power of silence is transmitted to the listening word.

Silence itself has this trust in the word and empowers the word to reveal that which is concealed in silence and which, at the same time, remains concealed. The logos, the word, is the translation of silence into the word itself. And this word is sonorous, meaningful, and effective in itself.

The Listening Man

The connection between silence and word is the same connection we find between impotence and potency. It is Advaita, Non-Dual.

Silence empowers the word and, at the same time, empowers Man who listens to this listening word, but not only listens but also lets it resound in him, gives it resonance and acts according to this word. And again Jesus: "That, which I hear from my father, I do."

This trust which rests in silence, this "do what you want" what the silence says, just is present. It is present for us, for our responsibility, and it is up to us to give an answer with our life. The trust which rests in silence liberates us and empowers us to this answer.

This Being-There of silence, which says nothing, which does not threaten, does not give orders and has no commandments and which has to be translated into the human sphere is the energy of the mystery. And the power of mystery is human freedom and human dignity.

People are hardly conscious of this, and we do not experience this power, freedom and dignity because we have allowed language to become so corrupt that it is only a means of exchanging signs, so that I can do something or know something. Our language no longer testifies and creates because we have torn words away from the realm of silence and because the listening word does not find resonance in our rigidity and narrowness. We no longer hear it, the sound of the living word.

The Incarnation of the Word

Man can hear the word or not. We can hear the message of the living word or simply cannot hear it. Not hearing, not only because of our bad will, but not hearing because we are deaf; not hearing because we do not pay attention, not hearing because we are distracted; not hearing because we are listening to too many other noises at the same time.

Listening is an art. And this art is designated by a word which I scarcely dare to name because it has been used and used up in an abusing false manner. The word which stands for the art of listening is obedience from ob-audire. Obedience means to hear attentively, to hear precisely—not only the words of others who are the same as I am, but rather listening toward the silence which is everywhere but which means only for the loving listener a revelation.

And how do I hear? I hear the word while receiving the word. And this reception is incarnation—the word is received in deeds.

In a human manner this reception is a repetition of that which, as I assume, has been preached in churches since they were established: "And the word became flesh." This is not the privilege of Jesus Christ. This is the fate of every person and of every word.

In many baroque churches one can see on the paintings of the annunciation how Mary received the Holy Spirit through her ear, in order to make it plausible for us to understand that we also can receive the word—even men and not only women can be 'conceived' by the word since we all have ears.

To receive the word and let it become flesh in us and thereby to become god-like, to become word—this is our task and this conception should be our answer. But, remaining in this metaphor, miscarriages can happen, and it can even come to abortions. This happens, to be sure, if the word disturbs me or frightens me because it empowers me to do something which I maybe do not dare to do or want to do because my life is entangled in so many noises of a vulgar existence.

Academically speaking, a misuse of freedom can occur. This happens when I understand my freedom to the degree that I give my whims full rein. Then I no longer have this obedience, this listening toward the messages of things and toward the messages of the others which have to pass through the filter of my ears and my conscience. They do not gain entrance because the filters are plugged. And the messages of life are blocked out and shut out and ultimately get lost. Virginity of reception stands here as symbol of willingness, of emptiness, of attention, of non-attachment so that we can become aware, in the right manner, of the birds, the trees, the sun, the cries of the little ones, the word of the lovers, or the admonitions which are also there. We should let all these things get into us through our filters, allow them to become flesh and work in us until they are born new and transformed.

These messages out of the immediate perception give us freedom and power. Without the freedom which lies in silent trust, there would not be any power. Power in the sense in which I use the word means the ability to use and not misuse energy. And again it must be mentioned that our words are sometimes a little atrophied because of misuse. Man can hear the word or not hear it. There exists a patriarchal characteristic of contemporary civilization, an attitude which is common to men and women alike. In this view the primary thing is to do something, to create something, to undertake something and to be busy instead of first listening to others, to receive and let it become flesh in us and then to give birth to that which was conceived. In this view prevails the excuse which says: I don't understand, I cannot do anything with this, I cannot use this for anything.

These objections exist. But they do not have to be a reason not to open and unlock ourselves in order to listen to the listening word and to be aware of silence and to resound in its sound because the word does not have to be understood, it has to be received.

The Sacramental Word

Using christian language I would like to say: the sacrament is the spoken word of the listening person. I do not speak of church sacraments although in church sacraments this power of the word is present. Let us consider marriage which is not only a christian sacrament. It is a sacrament in all cultures and religions. If one says yes or no, then this word effects what it says, and it changes reality. It transforms reality. This transforming mighty power has been stated in the decisive word of my first quote from the gospel of Matthew. It is the eloquent Greek word *αργον,(α-εργον), εργον,* deed-energy. A word, an idle word, which does not create, which has no energy, which does not transform and does not become deed, is no word because it is a useless word. And if this transforming power is not contained in our words and if they do not open life and beget life, then we will have to account for this.

What we have to learn is to listen, to receive, to allow incarnation, and to give birth in word and deed, just as we receive in word and deed. Otherwise everything we say is only superficial tittle-tattle and idle talk. Parents, teachers, and we all then complain that our words find no listener, that they miss their mark and have no impact. And the reason is only that these are not words, not words out of silence. They are words which do not come out of this incarnation, words which are not born in us. Then the listener senses that the speaker, the one who admonishes, does not live what he says, that he does not embody it—and then the word has not become flesh. Our life is our answer, and therefore every word from us should be a sacrament. This sacrament is the spoken word of the noble person, as Meister Eckhart would say, of the listening person, of the attentive person, of the loving person. And only the sacramental word in the above sense is genuine and true and has transforming and life-creating power.

The Power of Silence

Here the circle is closed. The listening person, the loving-listening person, the attentive person, the person in whom this incarnation happens, knows the power of silence which moderates and guides from afar. It is the power which guides things without commanding. The power which does not disturb the harmony but rather advances it because the listener, living in accord with it, wants that which has to be done; because the listener is not afraid to be extradited and has no fear that his way could take another direction than the one he had planned and intended; because the listener trusts.

But in order to listen, in order to take part in the power of silence we have to become word. We have first to learn to be silent, and in order to learn to be silent, we have to be empty. We should not have too many noises within us; we have to confront everything with such attention and devotion as if the past were gone and the future entirely unreal, so that I can concentrate and be a listener in my entire demeanor and activity and hear that which is to be heard.

This willingness, this fearlessness, this listening attitude, this obedience to the invisible and inaudible melodies of heaven, as the Greeks said the music of the spheres, as Pythagoras said, spoken in a christian manner, the listening toward the Father which we experience in the spirit by having realized the reality of Christ as word and having become son or daughter—that is the human wisdom and this is the power of silence. It is the power which is grounded in silence but does not lie in silence itself. The silence by itself has no power but silence teaches us to present trust, fides, faith in the word.

We have to pay attention to this incarnation which happens in us. And if we are attentive and are aware in this manner, then the word of the listening person not only has power, it has something else for which we usually are not prepared because we have let the truth freeze outside and have not prepared a dwelling place for it. The words of the listening person contain truth whereby the truth is neither my subjective conviction nor an objective correspondence in the sense of A=B. The truth is realization. The true word realizes what it says because it translates the reality into the effect.

The genuine word is the bearer of truth. And so truth is not outside of us. It is that which I say provided that what I am saying is a real word. The real word is the cause and brings about what it says. And this is the sacrament. The listening person, the attentive person, and as I said in the beginning, the loving person, knows the power of the word because he also hears the impotence of silence.

What can we do?

If we consider the present crisis situations, interpersonal, political, economical, religious, etc., then we cannot help but turn to the demeanor of the receiving listener.

If we want to turn the existing crisis situations around and transform them, we need rather a feminine attitude, which in accepting that which it receives, at the same time nourishes it, lets it live and grow until the hour of birth has come, and the begotten can be born in a changed form.

In order to meet the need we have to make this attitude our own by becoming this disposition because out of this disposition we can find our way toward the experience of immediate awareness.

In the immediate awareness in which this conception occurs, we conceive in the Christian sense of the word, words of the logos, of the word—when logos is translated as word. We receive that vibration, that message, that light or that dimension of reality which will nourish us and make our lives fruitful. We receive a latent dimension of reality which is not yet realized. And in this conception germinates creative power and human creativity.

So the artist is someone who conceives what does not yet exist. And it is his task to give existence to that which he conceived with his life. But an artist is no extraordinary person. We all are artists, poets, creative persons. At least we are creators of our own life. Yet we have to become first what we already are. We have to become true conceivers and persons who know and are capable of action, so that we are able to let that become what does not yet exist. In the process of becoming that what we are we become creators of our reality because we enter into a creative dialogue with life. In doing this we recognize that every life is a creation. Every life is something which did not exist before. Reality is always in the process of becoming.

In dialogue we experience this transforming life-creating power in us out of which we can form our life creatively. We know at the same time that in us we have this power of silence which we necessarily need in the present situation of upheaval in order to achieve a radical new orientation out of which we can creatively transform the existing crises. And we know almost with certainty if we shut ourselves off from the transforming power of silence, the world is headed toward a catastrophe.

Our world, the world as we have erected it with our systems, is an unnatural world, and it is not only in upheaval, it is on the verge of collapse because it is no longer liveable and against life.

The necessary new orientation and the necessary transformation does not happen by making a few reforms here or there, rather the new orientation has to go deeper in the above-mentioned sense. It has to be radical; it must reach to the very root of life.

For that we have to center ourselves while tuning into the sound of life and vibrate with the sound of that which is inexpressible, everyone in his own way, because in touching the sound of that which is inexpressible, this mentioned reception happens automatically and the one who receives is fertile with his life. His words and deeds will be seeds which beget out of new life and which beget new life. Into his life moves this inner peace out of which all life emanates. A peace in which I can accept myself although I know my imperfection, weakness and deficiency. And this state in which I am at peace with myself is the first and the only possible step to give peace around me a chance to come to life. A harmony which gushes forth and which interweaves all creatures, thereby transforming our entire Being.

This begetting and becoming only happens in a loving person because one conceives in love and surrender. But we often are too egotistical, too egocentric for this reception to happen. Many times we are not ready to surrender and love because we are afraid to let go of that which keeps us prisoner in our present entanglement. It is the fear of the radically new which does not have a form yet. It is the fear of our freedom, of our life which is not yet realized, and we shun the responsibility to shape our life creatively. We forget that every life, also our life, is unique and cannot reoccur. We give no answer to life nor to that which destroys life. We have to be reminded that no life is exchangeable or can be neglected. Nobody can realize what has not yet been realized in my life. Nobody can give the answer of my life for me.

Spoken in a christian sense, our answer is the new creation which germinates in this realization. Its realization rests within us, the creatures. It is not only our task, it is also our dignity because in this creative activity God is involved. In God's creation we are the forgers, builders and artists of our life and of the life which is connected to us. Life is total freedom. We only have to be that which is present in the symbol of the immaculate conception: unconditional and immediate receivers, the ones who hear the impotence of silence, the ones who experience the power of the word and the bearers of a new, divine life.

Translator's Note: One of the challenges in translating this essay was the rendering of the German verb empfangen. The two meanings of this word are to conceive and to receive. I chose the translation which I thought would fit better into the context. Another difficulty was the word Ohnmacht which in English can be rendered as powerlessness or as impotence. The German verb zeugen I translated as to beget which renders the notion of a spiritual conception and spiritual rebirth better than the terms to generate or to produce. The adjective Christian was not capitalized upon the suggestion of Professor Panikkar, and the German Kraft was rendered as energy, as well as power. I would like to thank Professor Raimon Panikkar to read the translation and make helpful suggestions.

The Signs of Silence

Pedro Cuperman & Owen Shapiro

What is truly meant by silence in cinema? Is it possible, in cinema, even in silent cinema, to speak about silence? The term "silent," as it refers to the cinema, hides a subtle paradox: how is it possible that a communicative art should be identified as silent? Who, inside a film, can genuinely say "I am silent"?

In a notable scene of *Los Olvidados* (Luis Buñuel, 1950) a boy named Pedro is at work in a poultry field. He is one of Mexico's street urchins, the forgotten ones, now unjustly imprisoned in a juvenile correctional farm. Another boy brings a bucket full of eggs. Facing the camera that is also facing him, Pedro picks one egg, punctures it, takes it into his mouth, and stares with disgust. The egg is rotten. Enraged, Pedro spits at the ground and angrily throws the egg at the camera. And that would have been all, had not Buñuel sustained the shot, letting the splattered egg linger, spreading all over the lens, dawdling down the frame and slowly crawling out of view. Even the average viewer cannot help but recognize the non-diegetic trajectory of the egg, since what should have blurred the lens and Pedro's image falls down, out of frame, leaving the image unaffected by the momentary disruption. Buñuel has interposed between the lens and the egg a piece of glass against which the egg splatters. Without the glass Pedro's image and with it the whole shot would have appeared distorted. Had Buñuel cut the scene either just before or right after the egg hits the lens the scene would still have dislocated the diegesis but without questioning the syntagmatic unity of the text.

At first, what we have just seen could be explained as a surrealist eruption, Buñuel quoting Buñuel, reminiscent perhaps of avant-garde's esthetical penchant for structural upheaval. As it is, the center of attention has shifted from the glass and into the viewer's semiotic space. One could identify this procedure as a typical (Baroque) incursion into our space, to tell us that cinema, like a dream, is also a reaction against a clear well-constructed everyday world, and that no amount of constraint can close the gap.

But there is something else. An event of this kind operates as a material intrusion that has little if any narrative input because it has no incidence on the plot. It could be described as a narrative lapse of which the accident is perhaps the model (an absurd statement, considering commercial cinema's highly editorialized character), or as an inside joke, addressed to a small circle of viewers "to share in the game of hints and omissions."[1] Or given the power of a cinema to formalize naturalist/realist codes, as a pause, or a break that can be read socially, politically, psychologically as commentary on the events, in the manner of the chorus in ancient tragedy. Or, as we would like to propose here, a lapse has a metaphorized implication of silence itself (John Cage's kind of silence, a silence that grows below or above language, a semiotic absence of signification, a linguistic void).

Another kind of silence, the one we have in mind when we say "silent cinema," is connected to socio-historical circumstances. It is made possible by a rhetorical ellipsis, by a removal due to a technological lack that produces silence: the privation of sound. But this is only half of the premise that guides our work. The other half (and we will present it here, before we examine the range of rhetorical forms by which the sensory experience of sound may be removed from the film text) is of a phenomenological nature since it involves the nature of perception. It assumes that in motion pictures, shot and projected at 24 frames per second, there is an implied link, although not always perceived, between movement and sound. This link assumes a hearing subject. Movement at 24-frames-per- second, perceived as a normal psycho-motor gestalt, always implies the positing of sound (for the same reason that a close-up of a head, a synecdoche, is not decapitation but implies the whole person). Only through a technological (non-diegetic) imposition of silence, a techno-silence functioning as a restricting device, which we call muteness (the silence of the silent cinema), can silence be generated. In themselves sound and image presuppose two aspects of meaning production which are always understood as self contained. However, in the moving picture there is a constant exchange of messages from sound to image and image to sound which can be viewed as completing or reinforcing each other. If we wish to separate sound from image we generate a rhetorical trope that is identified by an absence. We can describe this trope as an ellipsis, a syntagmatic omission of a perceptual character. It is a construct, a device like any other filmic device that announces or modifies meaning. Cinema itself is a mega-trope that represents a continuous movement via a contiguous set of juxtaposed images creating a perceptual analogue to natural perception. And, as in natural perception, any displacement in space is implicitly perceived as entailing sound, whereas its absence is perceived as an external imposition of a lack, muteness.

Silent cinema is an example of that muteness. Be it Griffith or Micheaux, *The Birth of a Nation* or *Within Our Gates,* silent cinema implies an ellipsis. The viewer cannot avoid positing sound to any perception of movement. The viewer perceives the sound as an absence, an absence that is perceived as gestalt, as a presence, and fills the gap. "Every consciousness posits its object"- writes J.P. Sartre - "but each does so in its own way. Perception, for instance, posits its object as existing. The image also includes an act of belief, or a positional act."[2] To assert the non-existence of an object (one hears an echo of Heidegger's notion of negativity) one must posit its presence as negativity, as absent. In the moving image silence is an indexical sign standing for the sound we know to be present as absent. Silence is cinema's mega-negative.

Within the realm of the silence-sound polarity we can identify a mediating notion of silencing. Silencing takes an external real event as a quantity of sound and reduces its volume, its value, in a way, its appearance. Silencing is neither the ellipsis of silent cinema nor pure silence. Unlike muteness and total silence, two quantitative concepts, silencing is both quantitative and qualitative, and it refers to gradients of change in sound, serving as indexical signs for that other paradigmatic silence. Among the varying forms that filmmakers use as indexical signs for silence we have isolated three that could help us understand how the polarity sound/silence operates in the cinema.

The first form we would like to describe as the sudden dropping out of sound, meaning the creation of an invasive audio gap—lapse—analogous to the visual gaps —lapses—of *Los Olvidados.* In *The Graduate* (Mike Nichols, 1967) there is a unique moment in which silence is marked by a change in music. In the often-cited segment in which Benjamin's affair with Mrs. Robinson is developed through a match cutting (keyed by a close-up of Benjamin against a black ground whose shape is revealed to vary from such signifieds as headboard, pillow, and chair), back and forth from Benjamin at the hotel room with Mrs. Robinson to Benjamin at his home, the sound track suddenly disappears except for the sounds of a door closing when Mrs. Robinson leaves the hotel room and a "splash" when Benjamin, near the end of the segment, dives into the family pool leaving only the Simon and Garfunkle music. The fictional time that passes, April to December, is implied by the second of two songs heard in this segment, "April Come She Will". Benjamin, seen in close-up, is reclining against a black headboard drinking from a can of Olympia beer, when the first song, "Sound of Silence" ends and "April Come She Will" begins. The split second gap between songs marks the moment as a lapse in the ongoing diegesis, and as in *Los Olvidados,* it breaks the narrative as it acts as a self referential, or meta-fictional moment by calling attention to the artistic construct (in comedy this self- referential event is coded as normative, but in naturalist/ realist drama it is a deviation). The lyrics of these two songs serve a prismatic function in relation to the image. As the camera focuses on Ben's gaze the accompanying music becomes a description of that gaze, Ben's thinking about his relationship with Mrs. Robinson. Thus, music functions simultaneously as mood and chorus, for it foregrounds character ("Sounds of Silence") and, in time, migrates to acquire an external point of view of the chorus ("April Come She Will"). The music is no longer a psychological element but a warning of the future, for the chorus always presents a futuristic event. These two songs condense time and narrative. The narrative structure is that of the daydream; vacillating between the daydream and reality are the eyes, or, if you prefer, the gaze of Ben.

*

What are those eyes thinking? Are the lyrics his internal story told from the point of view of the gaze, a sort of inner perspective, a point of view isomorphic with what in literature is known, since Charles Bally, as the free indirect?[3] Have we entered the head of Ben, a sort of *Last Year in Marienbad* reminiscing, without giving up the authorial position? In this segment the "Sound of Silence" is the story of the dreamer, while "April Come She Will" annotates the film's diegetic development. Thus, there are two types of condensation here, that of the daydream which can be read as character, and that of the time and space of the film's discourse. Though we cannot readily identify the syntagmatic nature of this structure (is it an episodic or ordinary sequence, or an alternate narrative?), no matter how we may postulate it, the moment of lapse, the gap that separates the two songs, produces a metadiegetic event.

The second form of silencing can be found in the oscillations between loud and quiet sound, an example of which we can see in *The Stalker* (Andrey Tarkovsky, 1980). The stalker is a man who leads two other men, known simply as "the writer" and "the professor" to the center of the outlawed region called "the Zone," where a mystical room effected by unnatural forces can fulfill man's greatest desires. There is a segment in which the three men, escaping from an advancing group of soldiers, obtain a motorized rail handcart. As one of the men starts the motor he cautions the others to be silent if they are fired at.

The scene consists of eight shots:

1) An extreme long shot that shows the men
   a) Obtaining the rail hand-cart;
   b) Filling it with gasoline while being shot at;
   c) Climbing aboard and leaving the abandoned warehouse-like building that is the place from which their journey begins.
2) A close-up of the writer facing screen right as he asks whether the soldiers will come after them. Another says they won't because they are too scared. When asked of what, there is no answer. The camera pans left, away from the close-up, to the land scape ahead of them, as if following the direction of the writer's gaze.
3) A close-up of the professor, also facing screen right, replacing the head of the writer. He turns until all we see is the back of his head. The professor eventually completes the 180-degree turn to face screen left, as did the writer. The camera then pans to a close-up of the stalker who also faces screen left then return pans to the professor who again turns his head, first into a right facing profile, then to where we see the back of his head, and finally, once more, to his right facing profile. The camera pans to the landscape.
4) The writer's head faces right and is downcast.
5) The stalker facing screen left.
6) The beginning of the fourth shot is repeated, showing the writer's downcast head lift up and slowly turn until he faces screen left.
7) Supposedly, a point-of-view of the writer looking at the landscape as the cart comes to a stop. The sound track becomes quiet as we rest on a tilted electrical pole that looks very much like a crucifix.
8) An extreme long-shot of the men on the cart in front of the pole. The placement of the three men, relative to one another is now clear. The writer is in the middle, the professor to his left and the stalker to his right as it is announced, "Well, we're home."

What is of particular interest in this scene is Tarkovsky's sound/image construction. Once the motorized rail hand-cart leaves for the open spaces of a passing landscape the gas motor's sound disappears and is replaced by a repetitive, ostinato sound, supposedly the cart's metal wheels over the track. Traditionally this device is read as mood. But, in the cinema, sound produces, among other things, a redundancy effect, which is a linguistic mechanism that in any language makes it possible to predict or anticipate the completion of a syntagmatic movement. The cart segment in *The Stalker* is, from the point of view of sound, a perceptual mystery. Its repetitive ostinato format reinforces continuously the mimetic and yet concealed side of the image (since the image here does not produce a sign referent for the sound: the wheels, the cart). The mystery has no easy solution, since the sound we do hear replaces (in our mind) that image, thus introducing narrative growth via a synecdoche. Finally, narrative content, previously carried by the image/sound binary structure, is now carried by the sound. The contiguity between image and sound forces a fundamental reversal in Tarkovsky: where before it was the image that informed us, now it's the sound. The obsessive repetition of the wheels on the tracks is more meaningful than the visual content of the segment.

The Stalker goes even further. The cart segment is of a substitutive nature: the sound that we hear is not what we think the actual sound should be. The mismatched directions of the character's facings and off-screen glances generate a spatial disorientation that is made comprehensible, as signifying the movement through a passing landscape by the ongoing audio track. As the segment progresses, these rhythmic sounds are slowly and subtlety over-dubbed with electronic sounds, whose rhythmic and orchestral construction reminds one of Ravel's *Bolero*, until, near the end of the cart's movement, the only remaining sound is electronic.[4]

We hypothesize that throughout the sound track what we hear was of a symphony nature, a concrete "Track Symphony." The images of the close-ups of the three men on the cart are set against the blurry shapes of the passing landscape. The sounds, connoting bumps on the tracks, supported by the bouncing of the image are never in synchronization, calling into question the relationship between what we hear and what we see. When the cart stops, the sound track is silenced. Only very low level ambient sounds remain until dialogue breaks this apparent silence, switching back again to the image as the carrier of the narrative. Then, the meaning of visual location clarifies and the men begin to discuss the place at which they've just arrived. This new "silence" marks the return of the image and sound to its traditional place.

Tarkovsky returns again and again to music and the critical role it plays in the cinema: "I don't believe films need music at all. In every instance, music in cinema is for me a natural part of our resonant world, a part of human life. Nevertheless, it is quite possible that in a sound film that is realized with complete theoretical consistency, there will be no place for music: it will be replaced by sounds in which cinema constantly discovers new levels of meaning. That is what I was aiming at in *Stalker* and *Nostalgia*."[5] But the "Track Symphony" is irrelevant if it doesn't function, above anything else, as a musical score; music in this segment's diegetic foreground with the image its background. To create this reversal Tarkovsky simplifies the visual, making the degree of its plastic meaning minimal, thereby increasing its metaphoric input, a significant emptiness involving landscape (Russian landscape) and the solitude of its people. This idea is supported by the ostinato that functions like a heart beat, anticipating what will come next. We see the men, but not what they see. In a way, the segment evokes silent cinema, a cinema that uses music which copies the ripples of the soul in order to mark the segments of the plot, as coded narrative information and as mood.

The third procedure of silencing operates by fading out to zero. There is a place in *Andrei Rublov* (Andrey Tarkovsky, 1965) where, unlike the sudden dropping out of sound noted in *The Graduate,* the entire sound track gradually disappears. *Andrei Rublov* is the epic story of a 15th-century Russian monk and icon painter. Tarkovsky summarizes: "It is easy to see how ill-equipped Andrei was for this confrontation with life, after being protected from it within the rarified precincts of the monastery, from which he had a distorted view of the life which stretched out far beyond it, and only after going through the circles of suffering, at one with the fate of his people, and losing his faith in an idea of good that could not be reconciled with reality, does Andrei come back to the point from which he started: to the idea of love, good, and brotherhood. But now he has experienced for himself the great, sublime truth of that idea as a statement of the aspirations of his tormented people.[6]

The scene in question takes place as a young man is running through the woods, fleeing from attacking Russians and Tartars who are pillaging his village. After a long-shot we see a close-up of him leaning against a tree near a stream, looking screen right. He turns, to look toward screen left, then to the rear. We only see the back of his head. The next shot shows a Tartar bowman, facing screen left, shoot an arrow, which in the next shot enters the back of the young man who is now seen frontally in medium long- shot. As the young man runs into the stream, in slow motion, and therefore altering normative time, creating an implicit alteration of sound, his movement causes water to splash up toward the camera, hitting the lens in countless droplets. As he falls into the stream with a last sigh, the camera pans from the external point of view of his body to the stream. As the sound track fades to zero, it generates a subtle shift to an internal point of view, that of his registering his imminent death. As in *The Graduate,* we confront a sort of inner perspective, a free indirect whereby the character's and narrator's (camera) voices are merged into the character's perceptual space, in this case, that of his dying. There is a repressed shout that drowns itself into silence, as an ultimate meaningful act. When the pan passes completely by the boy's body, and only the rolling stream fills the frame, the quieted sound track increases in volume, leaving only the sound of moving water.

Before we examine the continuum that is "silencing", we need to recall the discussion of the perception of movement that has been ongoing since the time of Frederick Talbot and Hugo Munsterberg. Munsterberg theorizes that the impression of movement must have conditions other than the actual performance of movements.

"Seeing movement is a unique experience which can be entirely independent from the actual seeing of successive positions. It is produced by the spectator's mind. It is the main mental activity, not afterimages, that unites the separate phases in the idea of connected action."[7]

Jacques Aumont, drawing on both Munsterberg and Wertheimer, specifically Wertheimer's hypothesis about the Phi effect as related to afterimages from post-retinal processing of visual information, points out that the black intrusion of the projector's shutter mechanism "masks the edges of each image, stopping the accumulation of persisting images caused by retinal persistence. At each moment only the present screen image is perceived, the previous one erased by the masking. Perception of movement in cinema is based on the same mechanism as perception of real movement, successive stimuli that are fairly similar."[8]

For Munsterberg the emphasis is on mental activity as a cause for perception of movement, while for Aumont this mental activity is contingent upon similarities in the visual pattern display of successive images. For us, these are not conflicting explanations, for it's possible to talk about these ideas in reference to binary and dynamic movements. Binary movement is that of the film projector's mechanical operation causing an alternation between black and image as each frame is held, then pulled down (what is known as the pull down, or intermittent motion mechanism) while the shutter blocks the projector's light as the next frame is moved into position for projection (a double-bladed shutter interrupts each frame's projection once, producing a frequency of 48 frames per second thereby eliminating flicker). Just as 24 frames of image are projected each second, so too are moments of black. This binary, black/image is analogous to the electronic binary of 1/0 (on/off) of computer language (the difference being that while the number 0 is a pointer to the number 1, black is not a pointer at all but is nothingness, a complete emptiness of light information." As the durational relationships between black/nothingness and image reach a certain shortness of duration, the binary disappears, masked by the combined effect of quick shifts between black and image. For our purpose, all image information on the screen is registered perceptually as if freed from black intervals, as a minimal unit operating at the threshold between perception and sensation. Dynamic movement, what Aumont refers to as successive stimuli, is only conceivable from the perception of the subject's movement. In the case of dynamic movement there is a gradation from non-movement to movement , from the still image to a fast-moving image. Movement can be so fast as to become a blur in that the constituent visual pattern elements (size, shape, direction, attitude, color) combine into a single impression, like the color white in chromatics. Therefore, we can understand the black/nothingness created by those moments in which the shutter mechanism is pulling down the next image frame to be exposed by the projector as analogous to audio silence, a silence without religious or poetic appeal, a structural, semiotic emptiness. A techno-sign . This techno-sign of cinema's technology is the formal ordering of the reel disclosed (that is, concealed) from the viewer by a chimerical Gestalt in 24 or 25 frames per second. "Order, says Foucault: is, at one and the same time, that which is hidden in things as their inner law, the hidden network that determines the way they confront one another, and also that which has no existence except in the grid created by a glance, an explanation, a language; and it is only in the blank spaces of this grid that order manifest itself in depth as though already there, waiting in silence for the moment of expression."

The visual transcription of ordered movement, the moving image, has no immediate effect on us. Though we see this binary operation as consistent with dynamic movement of actual psycho-motor experience, we cannot see it in itself except in the case where the film's shots operate at mega-binaries. In *The Flicker* (Tony Conrad, 1966) we watch a display of shots, composed, at times, of very few frames. When these very short shots succeed one another, they produce an analogy for the black/image alternation of projection. However, the consequence of this mega-binary operation is the production of negative after-effect phenomena. Such an after-effect can be experienced, for example, by alternating between very short bursts of green and white, producing the opposite after-effect, red. This after-effect foregrounds discontinuity, exactly the opposite of the continuousness produced by movement perception. This oscillation between visual opposites operates more like sound than like silence in that it has material existence.

No matter what filmic operations are engaged, the binary/dynamic relationship of black(silence)/image(sound) to the performative reality of actual movement as perceived through continuousness of visual pattern displays from image to image cannot be separated. Thus we discover a fascinating analogy between silence and image in which, as we have stated earlier, silence is impossible so long as we perceive movement. To not perceive movement, to not perceive, is to see the black between frames, an impossibility in 24-frame- per-second film projection. Black is a perceptible phenomenon only when presented as a mega-binary, a "shot of black." Black, therefore, as a perceptible some-thing-ness, as the absence of image, exists as a place on a scale that points to the black/nothingness between frames. Likewise, silencing can be understood as being on a scale, represented at both ends, in which 24-frames-per-second is in the middle. At one end is the still of radical slow motion. At the other is the blur of radical speed. Slow motion is at the minus end that ranges from the perception of extended movement to gradient changes in the visual pattern display, that becomes so slow that movement ceases, such as in the stop-frame printing in the bicycle segment in *Sauve qui peut–Every Man For Himself* (Jean Luc Godard, 1979), or Akron (Richard Myers, 1970). At the opposite end, on the plus side, movement becomes so rapid that all we see is a blur that dissolves the autonomy of each frame into a concrete object. Perception cannot keep up with the individual differences in the pattern displacements between frames so that the blur reads as if it were a still image.

On the one hand, a freeze frame of a rapid movement appears as a blurred image, an abstraction. On the other hand, a freeze frame from slow movement appears as a still photograph of high plasticity, a figuration. These permutations—from extreme slow motion or freeze frame, or fast movement that becomes a blur, or a freeze frame from a fast movement that becomes an abstraction—create deviations analogous to silencing. Both are the supreme negation of movement, existing only as duration, which is the qualitative aspect of silencing. *La Jetee* (Chris Marker, 1962) the story of a man who volunteers for a time-machine experiment in order to regress in time and thus prevent his lover from taking off on a doomed airplane flight, is structured by still and stop-motion images. While the still images have only durational value, the stop-motion sequences are read as discontinuous movement. Both have duration. Stop-motion generates the impression of movement when the durational aspect of each shot is short and allows for connection to the next short shot, while the still images have a duration whose length erases movement. Interestingly, this relationship between stop motion and still images as connected to duration is analogous to the idea of short shots being mega-binaries for the black/image binary of 24-frame-per second-projection. So, we can now see that there are three analogous sets; the black/image binary, the flicker effect of mega-binaries, and the macro version of mega-binaries found in the opposition between still/blur images. All three of these pairings are, in turn analogous to that of muteness/sound, sound/silence, and the three manifestations of silencing.

So, to return to our question, what is truly meant by silence in cinema? Film began as a new medium that by necessity spawned the creation of new codes, new ways of story telling, and new combinations of sound and image languages that would soon become rule, canon: art. And there were reactions against those rules, those codes, against that sound and those images. Those codes were part of the history of Western art. And so was the reaction, the sense of questioning a way of making sense that can only be questioned by non-sense, that powerful commonplace of the 50's and 60's avant-garde, or a new sense which is the recognition that cinema is first and foremost a language, a Western language. As the history of the cinema marched on, the avant-garde's usefulness waned. The avant- gardes of the 40's, 50's, and 60's, became readily marginalized in America while in much of Europe they were seen as part of the normative discourse. Experimental cinema, which from the earliest days was instrumental in rejecting old codes and creating new ones, was in time silenced or co-opted by dominant cultures. This could be explained because filmmakers like Jean Luc Godard, Luis Buñuel, and

Andrei Tarkovsky framed their art around the contradictions and problems of their culture. And that culture became the avatars of their own work. While American society consumed its "threats" by placing them in the cauldron of apparent, though marginalized acceptance, some European and Soviet societies exiled or ostracized those it saw as threatening.

*

In 1950, Mexico provided a haven for Luis Buñuel. Surrealism was still there, somehow; the world was still seen through the sliced eye of *Un Chien Andalou and L'age d'or's* backdoor eroticism (sex as an alibi for illumination, or vice versa). But those experiments were now framed in conventional melodrama, conventional styles, in the rolled up eyes of the character Jairo in *Los Olvidados,* and the clutching hands of the crippled beggar in *Viridiana's* rape scene. Is that cinema's version of silence? Is that all it could offer, so far, against modernity, against its own technological inducements: a parody, a weariness, an exhaustion of communication (to rephrase John Barth's readings of Borges)?

When John Cage was experimenting with silence he was not only abandoning traditional music. He was abandoning a universe marked by Judeo-Christian cosmogony based on a double axial order: a syntagmatic time sequence on one hand, and a paradigmatic dialogical opposition on the other. Christianity, according to Martin Buber, condensed revelation into redemption. Biblical silence is traced around absence, the absent god, man, language. Cage was abandoning that biblical paradigm because he was shifting from a monotheistic to a monist ethos of the other, more precisely, to a kind of artistic *weltanschauung* whose final objective was a denial of time because of a denial of otherness. It was a shift from Jehovah, the elusive other, the "eternal Thou" (Buber), to Shiva Nataraj, dancer, seducer, the self-effacing and ultimately the self-destructive God. Like Kafka's prose, this second shift makes of meaning an impenetrable castle, a Chinese wall, a gigantic insect: what Nagarjuna calls "Sunya," Emptiness. Kafka's affinity with that obsessive circular dialectic has been and is the avant-garde's temptation of every age and every art. The cinema as art and industry is the exact replica of this circular repetitive obsession. With one exception: it can seldom keep quiet, let alone be silent.

1. Pedro Cuperman, *American Baroque,* (New York, Holly Solomon Catalogue, 1988).
2. Jean Paul Sartre, the *Psychology of Imagination,* (New York, Philosophic Library, 1948).
3. Charles Bally, *Le language et la vie,* (Geneva, Edition Atar, 1913).
4. This brings up a problem we are exploring in another text dealing with the role between cinema's imge and techno music.
5. Andrei Tarkovsky, *Sculpting In Space,* (Austin, Universtiy of Texas Press, 1994) p. 159
6. Ibid pp. 89-90
7. Hugo Munsterberg, *The Film: a psychological study, the silent photoplay in 1916,* (New York, Dover Publications, 1970) p. 30
8. Jacques Aumont, *The Image,* (London: British Film Institute, 1997) p. 31
9. Michel Foucault, *The Order of Things,* (New York, Random House, 1970) p. 20

THE APPLE MONOLOGUES

Marco Maggi

At the same time every day, for ten days, I photograph two motionless apples. An aged apple, engraved by me sometime ago and already shriveled. The other, a freshly-picked, plump, red apple. At first, the freshly-picked apple is conspicuously larger. During the ten days, the aged apple remains unchanged, unlike the freshly-picked one that becomes smaller and shriveled. The power of time imposes itself on space. The apple becomes a trace, a memory, and therefore unattainable. It would rather disappear than reproduce. I am a printmaker who does not make prints. I do not like to reproduce, I cannot reproduce mechanically, nor digitally what I make because neither the scanners nor the xerox machines are able to read it. I am presently doing a series called "Soft Plate" and "Slow Print." These are similar to engraving plates but made on aluminum sheets. The idea is to make some portfolios where the plate is the publication. This brings up the problem of representation. What is being represented, the print or the work, the product or the process? Well, here the apple doesn't solve the problem but in my work the plate and the final product are the same. They are represented reciprocally. Here, the apple is reminiscent more and more of the original apple. Reduction and reproduction are opposing processes, enemies. More than half of the apple disappears in ten days, it dehydrates, a halo of silence, an ex-apple.

Translated by Tania Mordwinkin-Dabrowiak

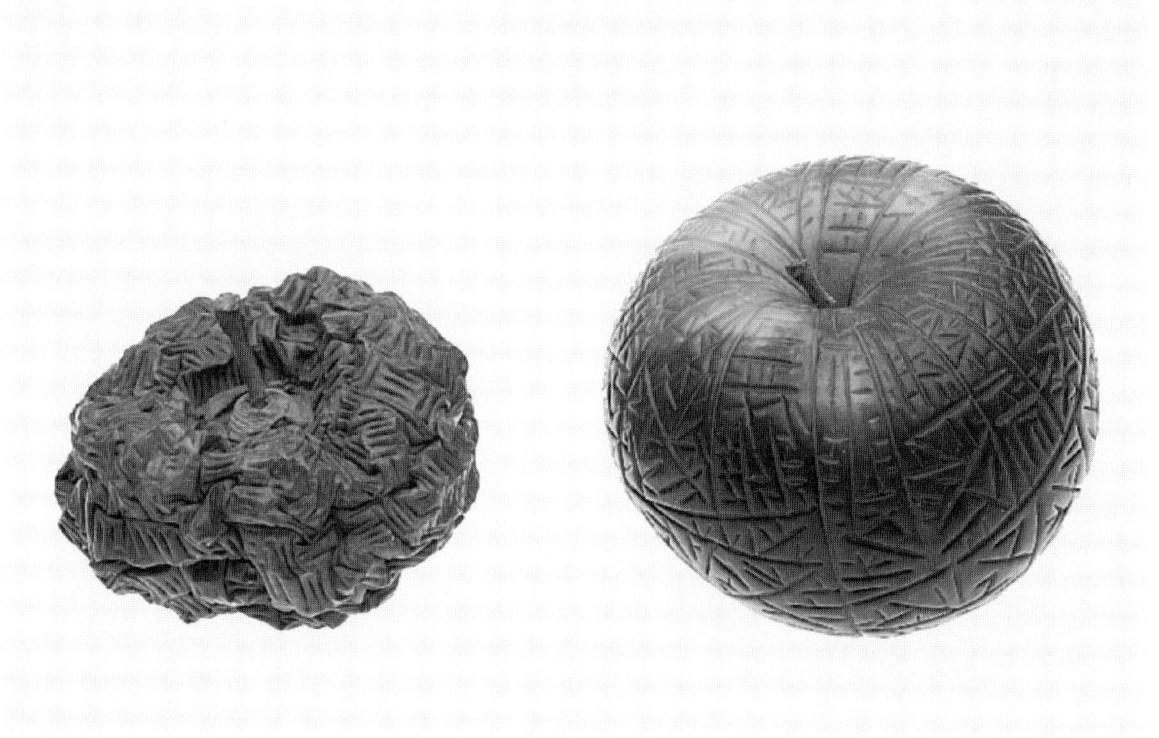

△ DECEMBER 23, 2000

DECEMBER 24, 2000 ▽

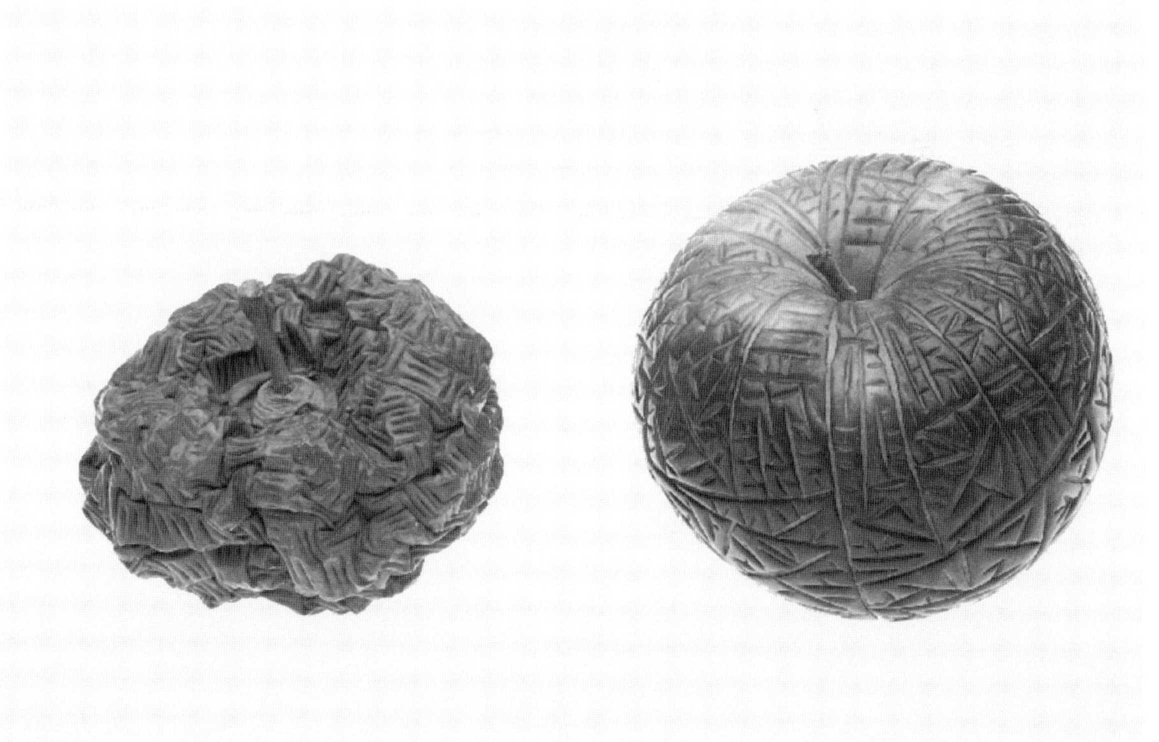

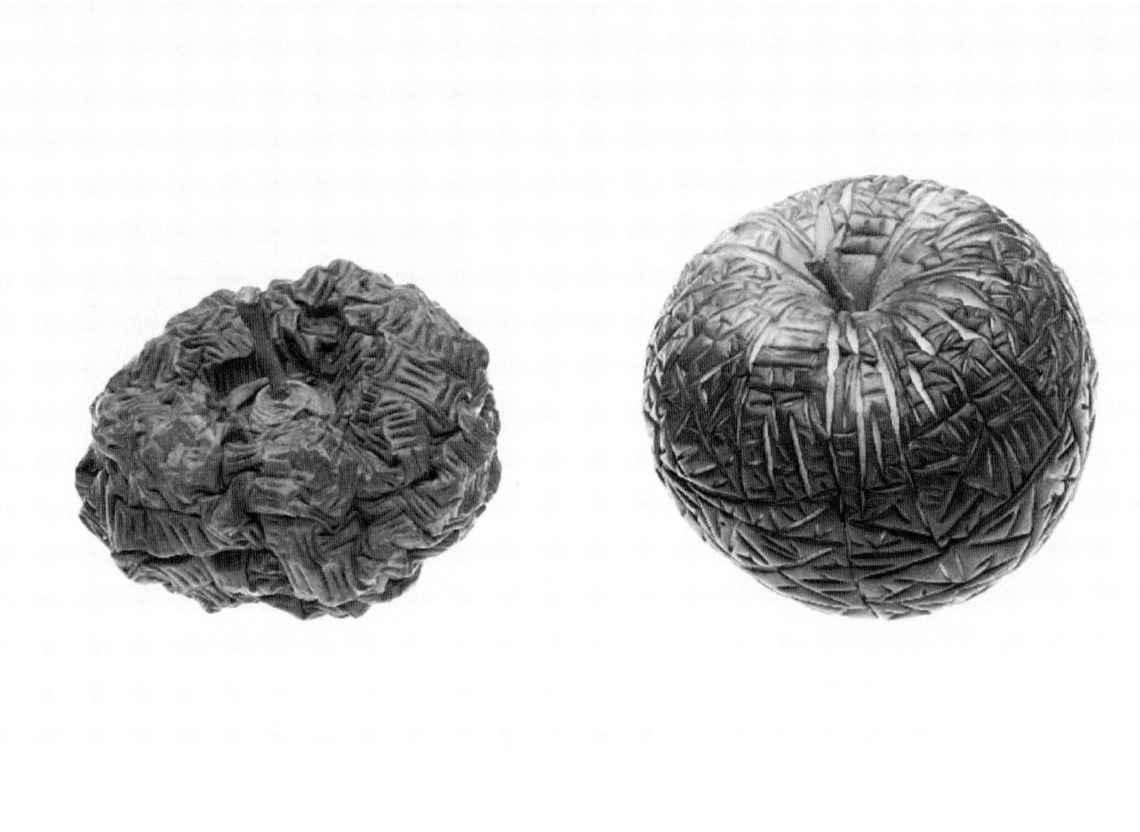

△ DECEMBER 25, 2000

DECEMBER 26, 2000 ▽

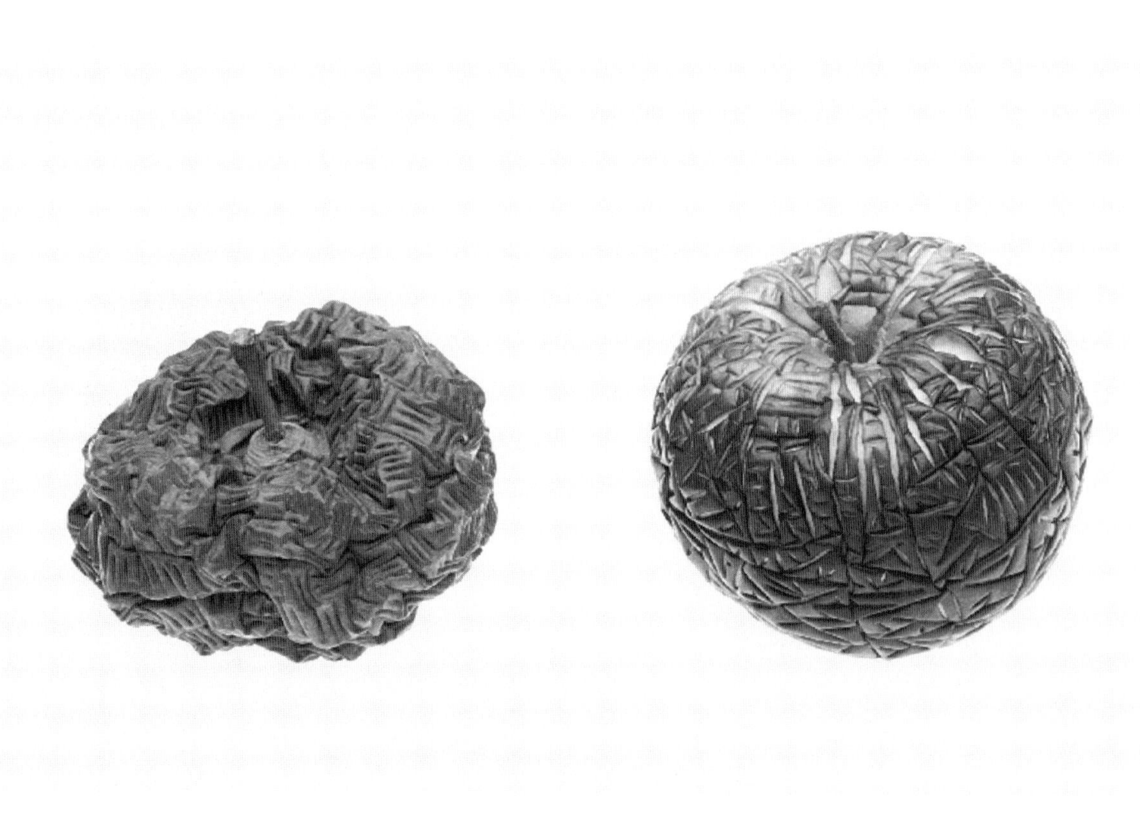

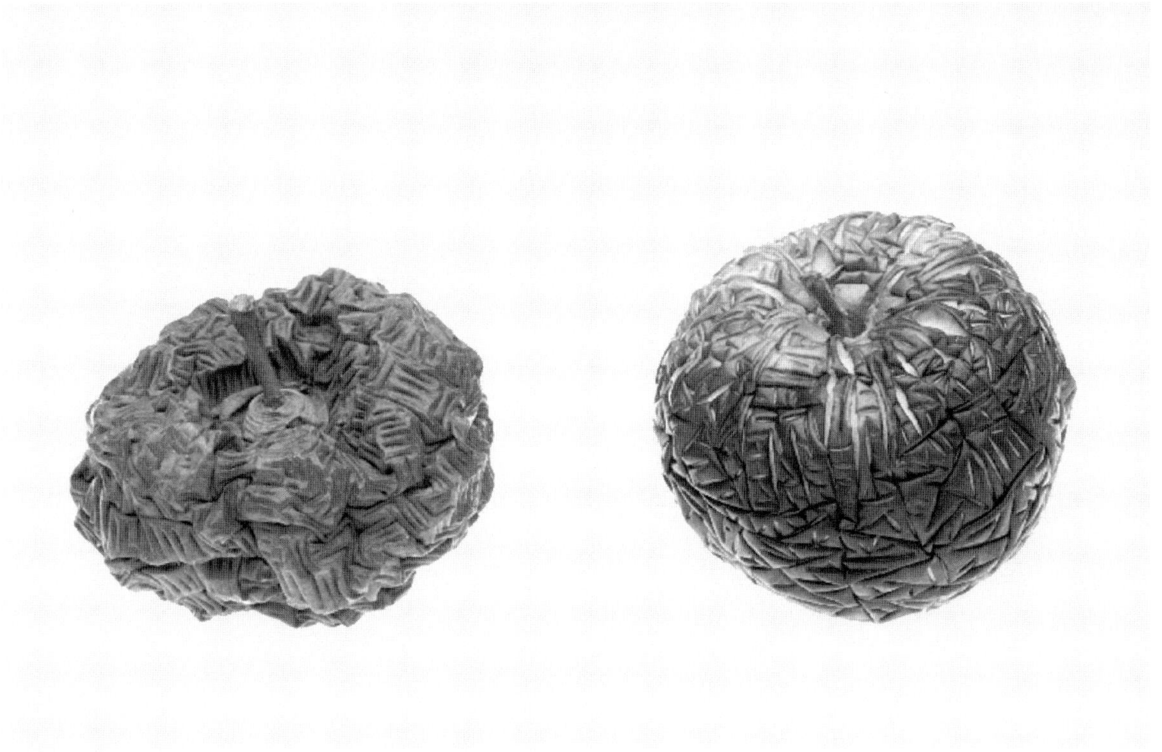

△ DECEMBER 27, 2000 DECEMBER 28, 2000 ▽

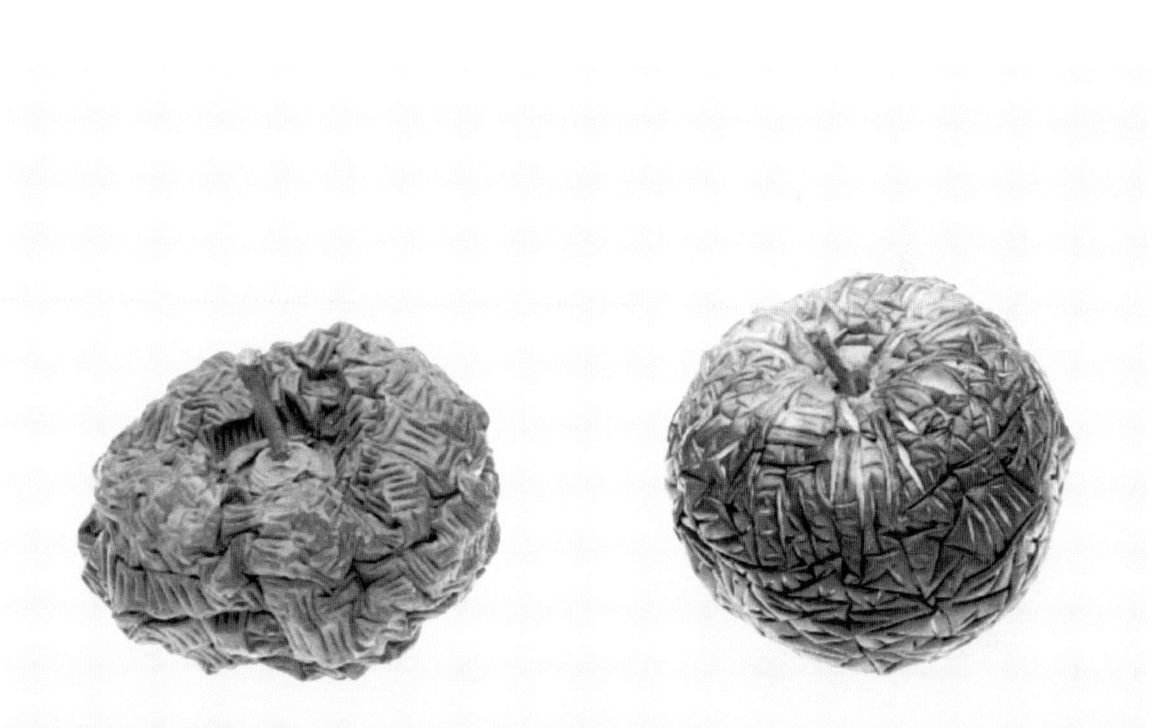

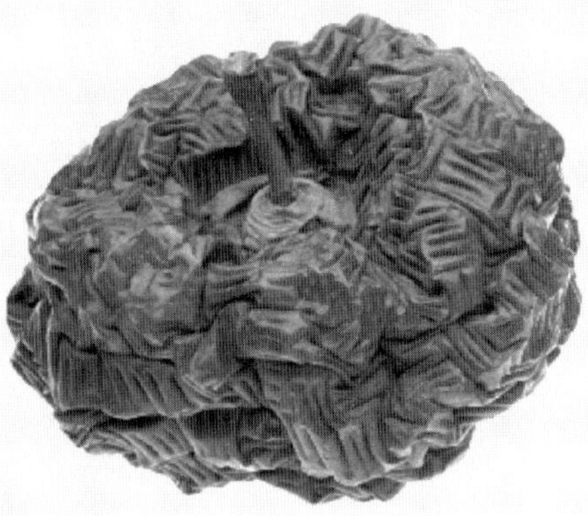

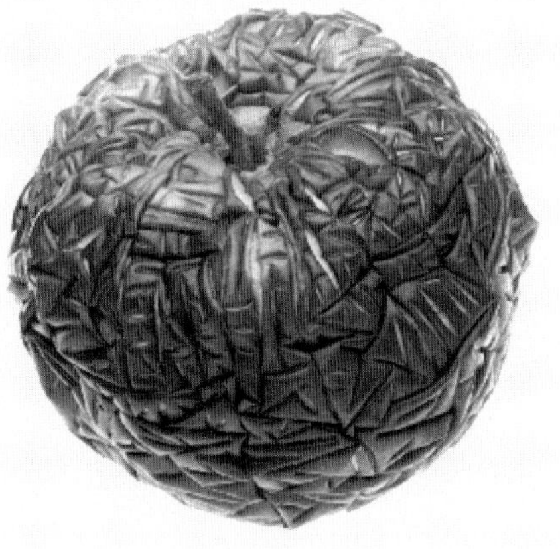

△ DECEMBER 29, 2000

DECEMBER 30, 2000 ▽

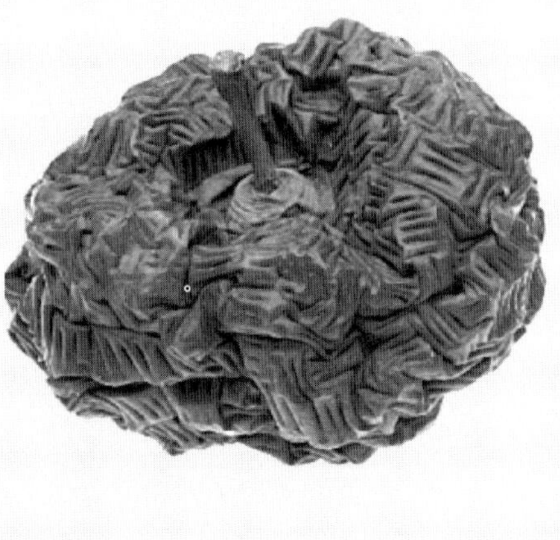

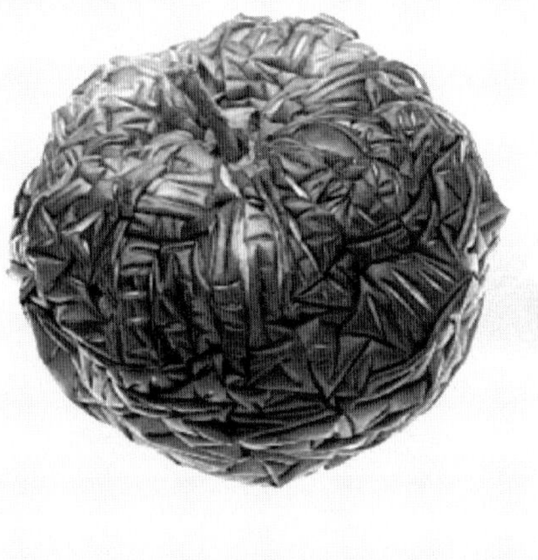

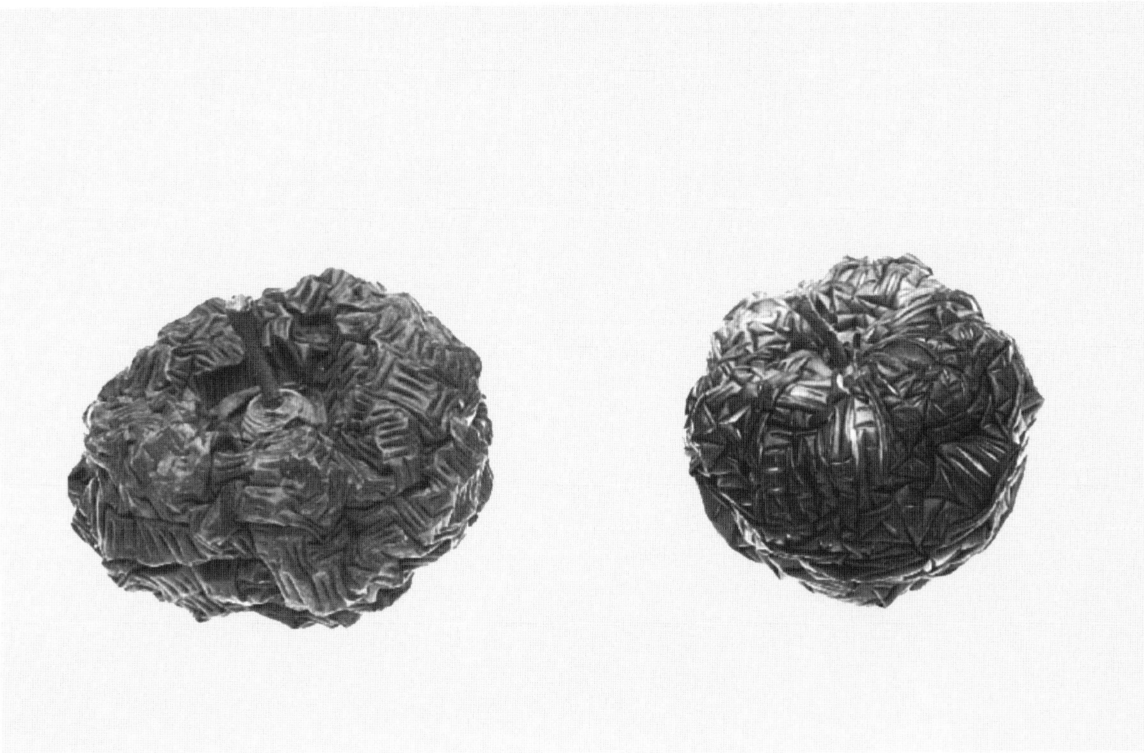

△ DECEMBER 31, 2000 JANUARY 1, 2001 ▽

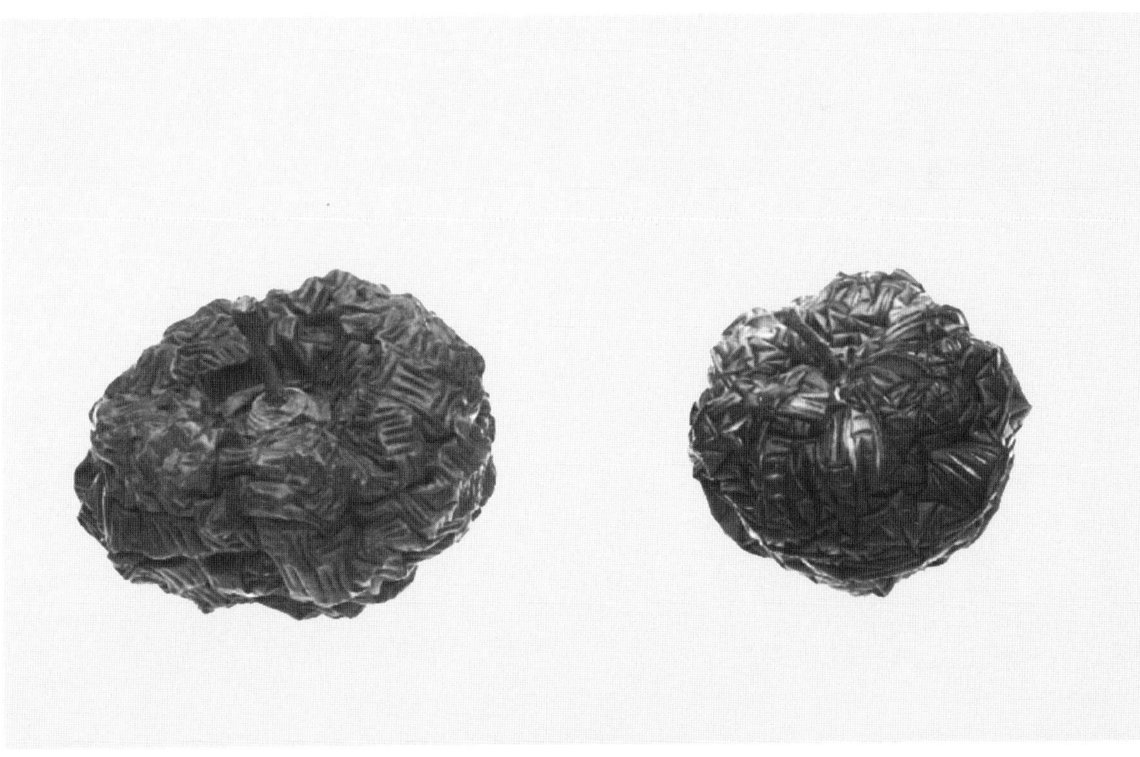

A Conversation with Trisha Brown

Pedro Cuperman

Dancing and writing. Why this conversation, this idea of having a dancer-choreographer talk to a journal that is concerned about silence? For us, for our journal, this is a rare privilege, for if it's true that dance and writing are, shall we say — arts apart? — we feel Trisha Brown very close to us. I mean that as a choreographer and dancer, through her body and her conceptualization, she brings forth a new line of thought, movements which we still can't name, bodily phrases that take us there, wherever that there may be, to a world that transcends our own closures. And that movement eventually shows us a new face of the world, our world, that in one way or another is also transcendence and closure. In Manhattan, at a very spacious loft, courteously eroding differences with this great American choreographer, we turn on the recorder hoping to talk about what, so far, we hesitate to mention.

C: In a story by Julio Cortázar a man walking in the streets happens to find a human heart, and it is still beating. The man wraps the heart in a newspaper and takes it to the next police station, where he asks for a receipt. I recall seeing your Walking on the Wall and rejoicing at your dancer's rare gravitational skills, spreading arms and limbs like tentacles in that most improbable of actions, walking on a wall. Later the idea struck me that the effect of that piece on me was close to the one I had experienced reading Cortázar's story. It was that same play of defying logic and all its implications without lashing art's tail. As we decided to prepare this issue on silence, I recalled posing that same question when I saw the *Accumulations* series, where such silence is ostensibly one of the subjects. When you kindly accepted the invitation to participate and asked me to come to your place I thought it would be a good opening.

B: Well, I can tell you why I did use silence. When after 1970 I was doing pieces like *Man Walking Down the Side of the Building*, and *Walking on the Wall*, etc., the sound of the environment, the ropes, the trolley, the gears, all of that was the music. It was the sound; It was the aural feel. It would have been an immediate association with Walt Disney if I had added music so it never came up. I never thought about music with regard to those works. The music was already there.

C: How?

B: The environment, the sound of the equipment.

C: No matter how mute the event, the music is still inside you, because you are a breathing rhythm.

B: It's true. There are the heartbeat and the breath. There is no silence. In the theater there is truly no silence. It is an audience filled with people. I have a theory that they become very anxious when they don't have their traditional music parallel to their dance, and they begin to cough.

C: So, do you incorporate the cough?

B: No. Actually every time they cough I think, "I could kill that person." There's a lot to ask of people who are not familiar with this way of thinking or to understand it, or to listen to it, as I do. But also, I work in cycles and I move on in choreography. After *Walking on Walls*, I went back into choreography more or less as we know it. That is, to use the stage, etc.

C: A frame?

B: A frame, and to join the circuit of touring, of dance. Otherwise, I was outside of it, and in trouble.

C: What would be the frame for the dancer climbing down the wall? Where are his or her borders?

B: My first answer is: the boundaries of their mind, of the audience members. The second has to do with the building: if you're walking down the side of a building I suppose someone could say next you're caught in the corners of a building. At the Whitney Museum we walked across one long wall and we turned a corner and we went on walking to end of a second, a shorter wall. You could dismount there, go down a ladder, and then come back up and go again. It was six people coming and going. That was the glory of the large white room, which is where I worked before I got into a theater. Those walls were of tactile relationship to the dancing, no matter where you were. We did bounce off it. We did go and touch the walls. In the theater you touch nothing. You touch into the wings. You're not supposed to touch the legs. If you do, crew members spank you. It's all illusional on stage. It took me a very long time to shift over from the surface of four walls to the absence.

C: In the *Accumulations* series you explored language, including the language of silence.

B: There were several that were totally silent. All together there were probably ten accumulations. I accumulated by taking, and I de-accumulated. The first one was standing, and it had music. Later I dropped the music, expanded the repetitions and added words, making it longer. The second, I was on my back, lying on the floor. There was no music nor word. I don't remember exactly, but before I added words—which I did—I stood there and accumulated gestures for ten or twelve repetitions for thirty minutes or so, in a minimalist zeal

C: Some critics in referring to your work use the word "postmodernism." This may sound naive, but postmodernism or what it meant until not long ago could be applied to many disparate things. In contemporary dance especially, one runs the risk of getting entangled in choreographic debates, which is to see your work only in opposition to modern dance.

B: The term "postmodernism" has been attached to me especially, and to many others. It is rather simplistic. It really means post Martha Graham. Let me describe a choreography. I had to explain myself vigorously during the period that I was working in silence. I learned a lot working in silence. Not only because in dancing along with your colleagues in an ensemble you hear them and you see them and I was working with some improvisational options so that one had to keep one's fellow dancers in view. So you're using all the senses: hearing, seeing, feeling. All the time you were performing during those periods. It was terribly human. Maybe terribly is not the right word. It was wondrously human.

C: I like that: *Terribly Human*. A nice title.

B: Yeah!

B: During this period, I learned how music colors dance. I was in every piece, but still I had to step out to see what I had done, as best as I could. I saw the movement, it looked as it did when I made it. I thought more about it. Then, music was added and it truly looked different. It is a very important idea. It means that music and dance–either language can alter, diminish or exalt the other. They are manacled to each other in a more complicated way than traditionally has been thought. I don't know if this is the right image: a tap, just a tap of the kaleidoscope can change the field. That began a period of working with and without sound. I myself could color the movement. I could change it. And it had everything to do with perception, which is out of my hands.

C: Which is what you are doing now, meaning in the year 2000?

B: Well, I keep going, so I can tell you more about it. I'm working very specifically with large western music masterpieces. It is truly interesting, and then most recently with jazz. So here we are, it's a raucous world. At any rate, going back to talk about that period, I made a piece I called *Foray Foret*. It belongs to the *Back to Zero* cycle of works. At that time I was hoping to separate movement from will, from conscious control. What do I mean by that? Simply to let go of the gesture selector we dancers carry inside

C: You could tape it.

B: It was scary, and I felt embarrassed, but my dancers were intrigued and kept me going. They were wonderful in supporting me because I had no intellectual control over what I was doing. Talking about gestures, they were small, strange aberrations, mixed in with regular dancing, as I do it. Fissures. Did I see that or didn't I? She actually did that? Oh, it is hard to describe with words. If you saw it, you would see a million things and it would be different from what I described to you. And music, on the other hand, was a marching band outside of the theater, marching around the exterior of the theater. Not playing constantly and I had diagramed for them where they could go and when they should play and not play. It was really a gift to the audience to deal with time and space. First of all, you hear a marching band and you go back to the parade of your childhood, or the football game. So there they go, bye-bye the audience! Back somewhere. Then on the stage is this dance which is organized and taking place but working with very small details. If you catch onto it, the difference between J. Phillip Sousa and those "small aberrational details" is the name of the game.

C: Always oppositions that bring forth some measure of clarity.

B: And obfuscation.

C: So in between is the fissure, yes?

B: Right. They could enter into hearing a choreography outside or they could see it inside simultaneously. The perception ranges of the viewer opportunities were vast.

C: Do you think that the viewer experienced the same kind of fissure?

B: One woman came to me and said, "you know the most amazing thing happened. There was a fanfare outside the theater. You should think about using it."So she didn't get it. Well, she got it but...

C: She got the outside aspect of it.

B: Yes. That has to do with what you see when you hear music. It is true that if you're ever in choreography just go like that because the music so often supports the dance or replays the dance.

C: So it is the "Ulysses" plight. The shadow of the sirens is always lurking behind the scene. How do you overcome that problem, by closing your eyes?

B: I don't know how you could do it. I can just turn the sound off in the studio and see the change take place. Music is powerful. Music can travel anywhere. It enters you, it enters the audience in no time and they blink. From the audience point of view the music is constant and full and edible. Whereas the dance has claims on their focus, their concentration, their knowledge. That's more difficult, I think. Not everyone is literate in dance. We have that struggle, so if you have a known musical composition, then, even though in my abstract choreographies with John Cage's music, I can use all the strategies of Bach, or Webern, all sort of systems and canons, if the music doesn't tell them what I am doing, they don't know it. Without the confirmation of the music the dance is perceived as unstructured.

C: Contemporary art seems clear and easy to understand but it's full of safeguards. It's mainly non impressionistic. You have to know. Information stands in the way. How does anyone see a piece by Rauschenberg or Duchamp outside the context of Western art? Therefore, enter the art historian, the critic. Is that the case of dance?

B: Well, I think the figure of the painting is legible to anyone and, you know, there's a comfort about that, knowing what you're seeing. The one eye Picasso on top of another and from then on any strategy for distorting. This was the nice thing about performing a lot in France. In America we don't really have that kind of support for dance at all, unless it's the more commercial kind of dance. So, someone might see me in Los Angeles one year, and then see me seven years later and they can't make the leap unless they travel and see a lot, unless they know…

C: Or read.

B: Or work in a university dance department and know. There's a real problem. As with painting. We can have a film or video of a dance but it's absolutely not a substitute for a live dance. Whereas you get a recording of music and a published book and a published painting, or photographs and the experience change significantly. People can see it in a book, a museum. With dance...

C: Well, that's when Time and Representation become topics. A dance performance takes place here and now, and this means that it cannot be replicated. It will never be the same.

B: Yeah, absolutely. We have documents of our choreographies for teaching purposes and many people will ask, "Do you have a videotape? I'd like to look at it." And I just hand it to them and I have to because that is the only way we can substitute the actual performance.

C: It's like talking about the unconscious but not letting the unconscious do the talking.

B: That's right.

C: A true challenge.

B: It is, and it's part of the elegance of dance. To record a dance on film or video you have to open wide to encompass the whole stage. But when you're sitting in a theater looking at a dance, I go to a section in this field of activity and I play with that all the time. It's one of my most favorite games. Sort of a "Did you see this?" The eye goes where it wants.

C: A paradox?

B: I thought of it more as a gift to the audience: that you have more to look at than you know. It isn't all on stage. I've been very interested in what people see for a long time. I'll give you two examples, one is from *Set and Reset*, that piece I did in 1983. It had a score by Laurie Anderson and set and costumes by Rauschenberg. Basically the construction is a dance phrase that goes around the outside of the stage space and it's like a conveyor belt that delivers duets and trios into the center, and then picks up and continues. What was the perception? I worked with visibility and non-visibility, which meant the dancers in the creation of the piece were told to disappear and reappear. Basically, they did it in different ways, lying down on the floor as an exit and staying still. They imagined they were out of sight, out of the frame of the theater. It's just an idea. Because if they are not exited, they are corpses. Otherwise, what are they doing there, lying down on the floor!

C: And could they be seen?

B: Yes! They were in full view. It's like a very sweet childlike thing. Then, during the process of composition, I would hang black velours in my studio. Dancers disappearing and reappearing. There were all kinds of calamities that went on in the wings because they would go blasting out and I'm not telling you the whole story on this so maybe you won't get it as clearly but I hope I can get away with this. Rauschenberg, when he saw all this energy in the wings, made them transparent. He used a scrim, so that all the behavior in the wings was visible, which made us uptight, we weren't our natural selves anymore. No more private sanctuary. Now we were on view, and it took some learning to come back and be more natural there. Different levels of being and not being, seeing and not seeing. Then, following that, about ten years later, I made *Astral Convertible*, also in collaboration with Rauschenberg. It was an experience in London. We were in a theater, the old Sadler. The balconies rise vertically into the heavens. I realized that the cheap seats, where all the young choreographers are, had an impaired view of the stage. What you saw was actually the floor, the top of the dancers heads, but not the backdrop.

C: Il Paradiso.

B: Paradise?

C: I think that's how those cheap seats are called in Italy.

B: Oh, that's lovely.

C. Poor people go to paradise, is the saying.

B: I think we call it the peanut gallery. Anyway, I thought about the kids who can't see the backdrop, the set. I made a vertical dance and a floor dance to function at the same time. The floor dance was the set I am delivering to two levels of vision: my aerial and my frontal audience.

C: A dance-floor?

B: Yes! There were beautiful designs on the floor. More like a filigree of endless activity, the dancers always working. They enter the space truly by powering up from the floor. They leap vertically.

They could be seen as two axises, the vertical and the horizontal, and they were interfaced. The kind of work that went on in *Set and Reset*: coming around, playing at the edge. By the end, I took the edge and moved it toward the center, and then I spun it. The whole dance rotated to all the axises of the audience vision. A line here is where the king sits and they don't get this gorgeous view, this venturing line. You rotate it one degree and these people have to be dah, dah, dah, dah..., and then it comes back. That's why I did that, to deliver the form equally to everyone in the audience and that's got me to the point of, how shall I say it? We're into perception here. I'm talking about perception. I think you wanted to talk about silence.

C: It's okay. You were very helpful in trying to describe how things move from being visible to being invisible.

B: Well it's been seen all over the world since then.

C: So actually it ended up being very visible. Now, going back to the past, during the 1960's there were a lot of explorations going on. Those were the years of the Vietnam War. What was the role of The Judson Church Dance Theater in your work?

B: Well, we had no place to perform. The Church had a Poetry Center and a Gallery where they performed Happenings. So it was natural to go there and ask if they had a space we could dance in. They said we could use the sanctuary. But we didn't go to church on Sunday. We stayed out too late on Saturday night doing the twist. Speaking about past stories, I want to tell you one about Bob Ashley. It's short, but it's one of my favorites. You see, I worked in silence and then I worked with music that was recorded and played over the sound system at the same time we were dancing. In some cases it was like live music, or recorded at any rate. As I first started using music, it came in sort of step-by-step and I went to Ashley in one of those early steps and I said — I forget all those details of what happened: but I said,— "Bob, this is really a big moment for me, I've never really used music before in my work." And he said, "Neither have I."

C: That piece you did in collaboration with Nancy Graves, can we talk about that?

B: Sure. No one ever asked me about my work with Nancy.

C: I'm curious since we did some work together.

B: Yes, I know you did. Ask me a specific question because my mind blurs in approaching talking about her.

C: I felt that Nancy's work, or at least the type of sculptures and paintings she was doing during the period was like a writer's dream, or nightmare, constantly thinking up new ideas out of some old discarded objects: palmetto leafs, marine instruments, coils, natural and industrial fragments to be recycled into art. Each piece grounded in a structure, that is, in a sort of logical order, a harmony that owes little to figuration but reaches its full stature in some colorful imagery, a recognizable perceptual event that in art history was and is referred to as baroque. To me she was doing exactly the opposite of what I tried to say to you at the beginning of this conversation. Segments assembled into a configuration which in itself makes sense, even if the whole is nothing more than the sum of all sorts disparate things. In your case, at least in works like Walking on Walls, I think it quite the contrary. Each segment seems in place, intentionally clear, geometrically precise, but the total perception is not, at least not something we met before. To me the power of the image is here, in that we didn't see it before, or at least I didn't.

B: I'd actually probably have to think about *Lateral Pass*, a piece we did in 1985. I haven't seen it in a long time. It is a choreography that has a lot of important ideas that didn't get fully developed by the time it was premiered. Those ideas went on to be resources for years.

C: Like what?

B: Broken patterns, making a travelling phrase, what you call a floor in dance class. Travelling steps is what you call it, a phrase which moves across a space. I was thinking about my childhood. I made Olympic National Forest Running fast through these changing surfaces on the floor as if it was moss and mud and hardwood and rotten wood. If you're going fast, you just have to pick where you place your feet. It is a child's first experience of running fast. But that it is not going to be your basic one-two-three/two-two-three/three-two-three. It was totally asymmetrical and unpredictable travelling patterns. It's an example of something I went on to explore later. It became a subject for me.

C: A kind of going to and fro, a kind of itinerary which seems consistent while the shifting of the ground is not...

B: Right, which may be a metaphor for the whole piece because Nancy's first idea for working on the stage was to have welders up on a platform and arcs of sparks coming down on the stage. Well you can't do that, and you can't do it around people.

C: The smell would be unbearable.

B: It was a beautiful idea. I wanted it with all my heart but I didn't have the staff that could make it work. If I were on Broadway I could do that because I would have the budget. But that was the thing, Nancy, it was her first piece in the theater and her first ideas were great, the best, and we couldn't develop them. Even the piece that she did finally make was too big and heavy for us to travel with. It was a ton of stuff, and you couldn't carry it. We didn't have the money to carry it. I was in my mid-thirties, trying to make a dance company. But you should see her notebooks. Her costume designs are just fantastic.

C: You have them?

B: No, her foundation has them. At the end I had to settle. I asked her to make sculptural costumes and that she did. She also made the funniest piece I ever saw in my life. She had panels of things hanging off people. I don't remember, snakes, maybe all over their bodies, pinned on... And she said they could change all the time. Well, people think dancers are very free spirits up there, but they're not. They're perfectionists, they're disciplined, and they don't want stuff flying around all over their bodies that might come off and take their mind while they're performing. They just want it clear and simple so they can dance, so the dance can come out. Nancy never... you know...If we had worked together one more time we would have something specific to refer to. But she died.

C: And now?

B: Well, I've moved into working with music, as I mentioned earlier, because I wanted to go back to opera. I had sort of a fluke of an experience with choreographing *Carmen*. It was wonderful. I think that the direction of the opera was mixed. I was more contemporary and the director was more filmic/dramatic. I was abstract and she was more narrative. It was out of this world. So I just had a ball. It was like a vacation on a magic island.

C: Where was it done?

B: At the San Carlo, in Naples, which is a historic, remarkable theater. It's as big as Mount Rushmore. I knew I always wanted to go back to opera after *Carmen* but it took me a long time. I did it in '98 with Monteverdi's *Orfeo*. And that's how I went back into Western music to make myself and my dancers accountable to musical scores. Can I brag? My mother taught me not to, so I have to ask permission from my father.

C: Permission granted.

B: Life is weird. It was hard work. I worked my heart out. I put my heart and soul into it. I've never worked with narrative and emotion and character. The world, I got the world out of this. It was extraordinary.

C: So you came back to narrative, fiction?

B: Yes I did. And I did it well. How can I do it well? How is it possible for me to do it well?

C: People think there is more than one door, actually two. One is tradition. The other is going through another art. Usually writers take from other writers and go until it breaks down, the same happens with painters, dancers, everyone seems to follow that way. But when you combine, or cut across another art, each one gets blessed or cursed by the other and it finally becomes narrative, the black sheep of the avant-garde.

B: In my case it was the filmmaker Lina Wertmuller. They called us six weeks before this four and a half-hour opera had to be choreographed. That is no time at all so we just took the repertory that existed, *Lateral Pass* being part of it, and said, "Okay, is this Spanish or not?" We just changed the inflection. In my case I accented my neutrality. What were you just saying?

C: About the narrative. That you finally came back to narrative. I think at the end a spectator or a reader or always makes up a story no matter what.

B: That's what it was. Character. Suddenly I was dealing with sexuality in my dances. Men and women, motivation within the human being, etc. So I began to play with the meaning in my abstract gestures, which had always been highly honed for neutrality and beauty, that kind of notion. I would play, and in the course of a sequence of gestures, I'd put in a human gesture that we all know, that we can all read. But then I would mediate that gesture by what came before and what after, so it was like flashing a card and they would see sorrow and then it wasn't there anymore, almost immediately. And did I see it or didn't I see it? And that kind of an edge was, I just kept going with that. By the time I got to the opera I wanted to tell a story. I didn't want to flash cards anymore. It was beautiful. There were parts of it that were just beautiful. I learned so much. It won the Grand Prix in Paris that first summer. It was born in May and it was anointed in July.

Leading Dance

Panayiotis Michael

An Interview with Ana Tiscornia

T: The more I see *Leading Dance*, your contribution to this issue of *Point of Contact*, the more I see the image of a dog chasing its tail. But don't ask me why.

M: *Leading Dance* is a drawing based on the sketches I did for the show *The Beauty and the Beast.* The original, the first set of pants, has been copied many times. These copies, these empty-unbuttoned pants, invite the viewer to put them on and join in the dance. That's how they adapt their behavior to the original.

T: And they go along with it; they chase their tail.

M: Well, what I'm generally really interested in is how things, ideas and ideals, thoughts, etc., get transformed into objects of desire, how they become the objects of consumption that are made daily for every taste and preference. I'm interested in how these objects take the place of others that have already been over consumed.

T: And in how such models go on to become models, no?

M: And also in how we usually adopt a model and follow its behavior. Maybe because we long to belong to something, to speak a "common language" so that we may be understood. I'm thinking now of Barbara Kruger's maxim: "I shop, therefore I am." Doesn't that show that she follows a certain behavior to prove that she exists?

T: Yes, but *Leading Dance* seems to talk about a specific form of consumption. What is reproduced is a pair of pants, a man creating himself, at once the reproduction of a model and of the individual transforming itself into the model inasmuch as it contains each one of its duplications.

M: I'm alluding to an obvious masculine stereotype, obvious at least in my country, Cyprus. I mean, we belong to the acceptable, we are not different. I like to examine the things and situations that surround me. This is how I discover new patterns whence I see myself.

T: At the end art is a tool to get close to yourself.

M: What we generally do in art is to examine what has engaged our thoughts. In the process of examining further we discover things, new things, and we react according to those new things and situations. I think that by way of our experiences, in art or in other realms, we usually discover new things about ourselves, things we didn't know before. And to that extent, art is a way of getting closer to one's self.

T: To what extent, then, are you the dancer of your own dance?

M: The answer is in the next drawing, maybe.

Translated from the Spanish by José Sanjinés

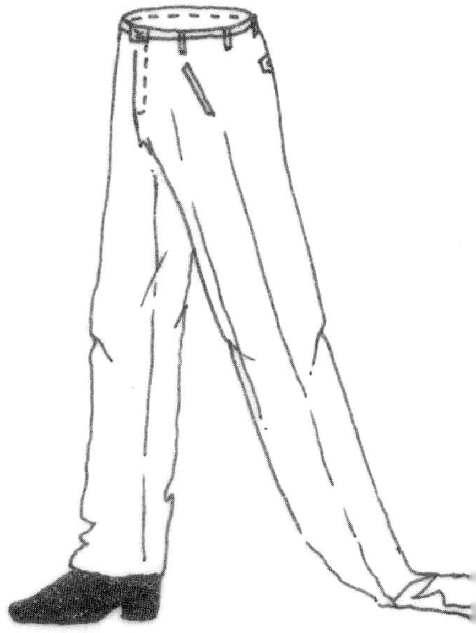

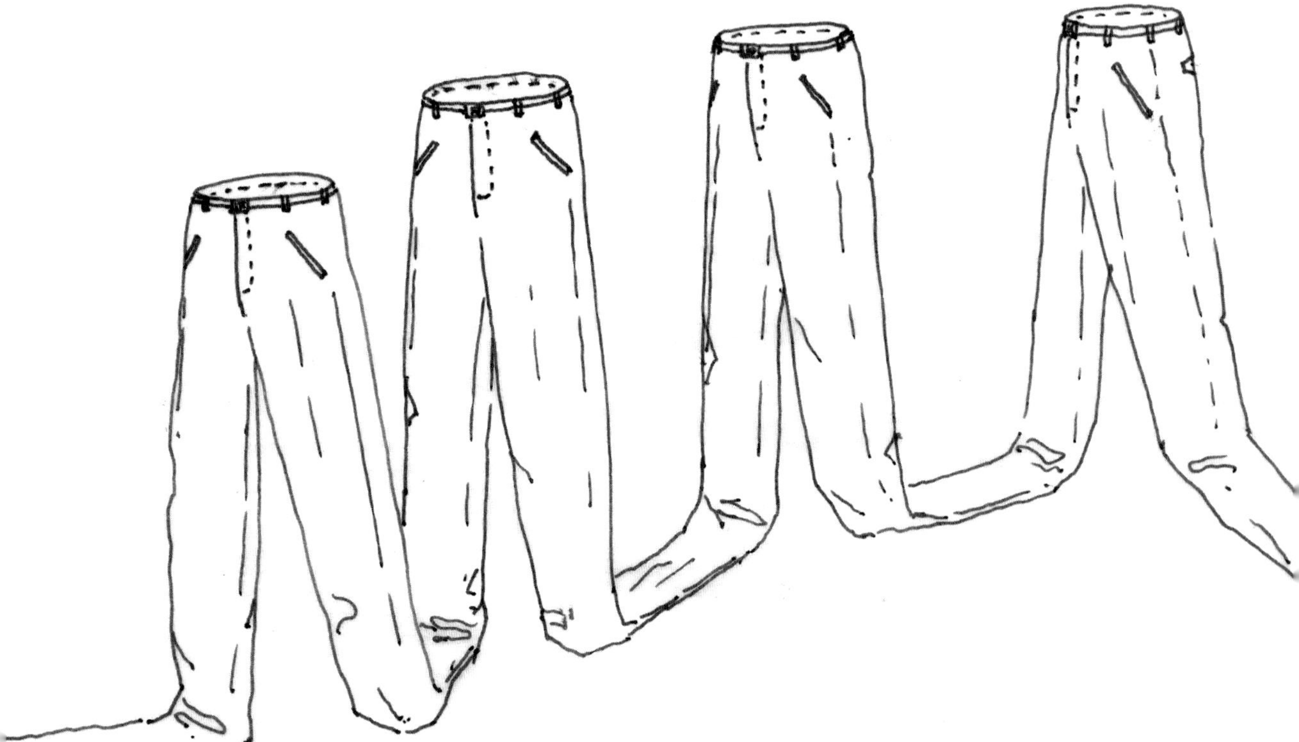

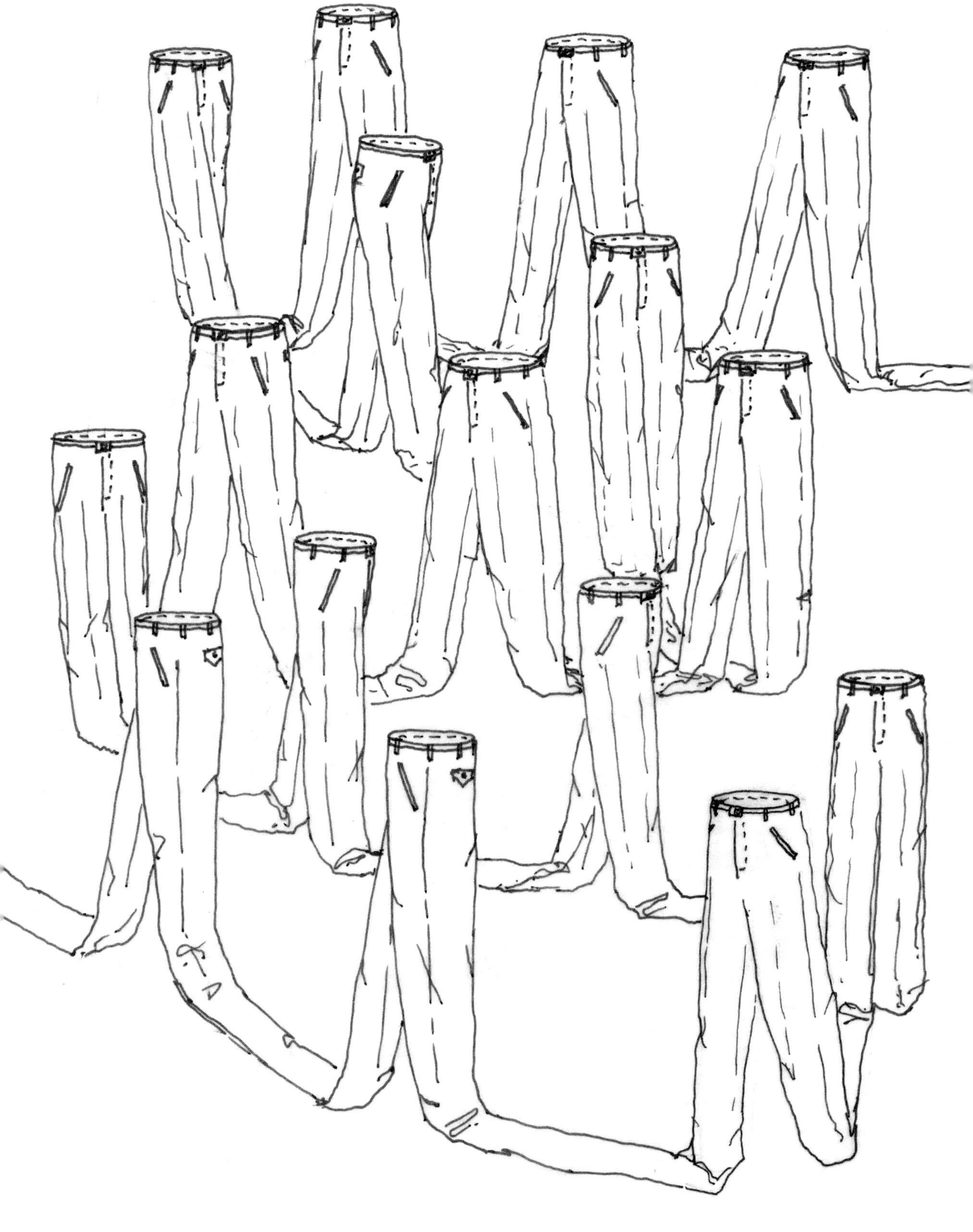

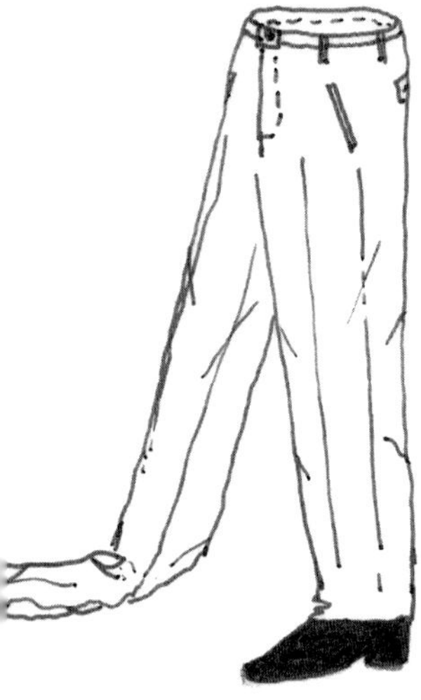

PANAYIOTIS MICHAEL

POETRY AND SILENCE: Valéry and Rimbaud

Jeffrey Mehlman

On March 7, 1914, André Breton wrote a letter of homage to Paul Valéry, who would receive him at his home on rue de Villejust a week later, thus intitiating a friendship that saw, among other things, Valéry serve as best man at Breton's wedding, in 1921, to Simone Kahn. For the historian of poetry, it would appear to be the oddest of conjunctions. For the heritage of French modernism, it is generally agreed, begins with a bifurcation in the Baudelairean dispensation. The poet of *Les Fleurs du mal* was simultaneously a neo-classical polisher of strict verse forms and an explosive prophet of poetry's mission to take us, in a phrase borrowed from Poe, "anywhere out of this world." On the one hand, the exquisite pressures of the Ile Saint-Louis, in whose confines he set up shop; on the other, the expansive possibilities of the Ile Maurice, the exotic island in the Indian Ocean he would never forget. That Baudelairean tension would not last. On the one hand, Mallarmé, then Valéry would pursue the neo-classical tendency; on the other, Rimbaud, then Breton and the Surrealists would pursue the will to paroxysm, indeed convulsion, without which, as Breton had it, poetry would not *be*.

How, then, did Breton come to court Valéry in 1914? The answer is that he was attracted less to Valéry the poet than to Valéry the ex-poet. It was, in a word, the *silence* of Valéry, intitiated in the course of a much heralded crisis of October 1892, that inspired Breton's cross-over to the adverse tradition. As he would comment years later in a volume of interviews: "In my eyes, he benefited, under the circumstances, from the prestige implicit in a myth that could be observed crystallizing around Rimbaud: that of a man turning his back, one fine day, on his *oeuvre*, as if, with certain peaks achieved, that oeuvre in some way rejected its creator."[1] The intertwining of the two Baudelairean strands was, then, more elaborate, more surprising than Breton's overture to Valéry in 1914 might suggest. Beyond the Breton/Valéry conjunction there was a fundamental--silent--resonance affirmed between Valéry and Rimbaud himself: two grand and, to all appearances, grandly incompatible figures joined in the salutary impact of their abandonment of poetry.

The paradox, of course, lay in the the fact that Valéry, to Breton's future chagrin, was, at Gide's behest, secretly engineering his "involuntary" return to poetry during the very years that Breton found himself drawn into the Rimbaldian aura of Valéry's "silence." "La Jeune Parque," Valéry's "involuntary *Aeneid*," was begun during the Great War, finished in 1917.[2] The extent of Breton's disappointment at what is arguably Valéry's greatest achievement appears, at its most succinct, in Breton's subsequent dedication of a copy of the Surrealist Manifesto: "A Paul Valéry, 1871-1917." Valéry, whose major volume, *Charmes*, would follow in 1922, died during the night of May 31, 1945.

We would appear to be confronted, then, with an embarrassing confusion, on

Breton's part, between the authentic silence of Rimbaud and the truncated and spurious silence--a case of *reculer pour mieux sauter?*--of Valéry. The matter is further complicated, however, by the specific resonances of Valéry's "silence" and its relation to the poetry that followed. To recall the circumstances of the poet's abandonment of his art, the so-called "Genoa night" of October 5, 1892: Valéry, a leading member of the young Symbolist côterie, abjures poetry as ultimately deleterious to Mind. There hovers over his decision a cult of Intelligence (whose emblematic hero is "Monsieur Teste"), of intellectual mastery, and, no doubt, at bottom, of mastery or power itself. A fantasy of Leonardo da Vinci would preside with some explicitness over the new dispensation, and I have suggested elsewhere that Georges Vacher de Lapouge, the racist craniometer and theorist of Aryan (or European) supremacy, in whose service Valéry, in his youth, had exhumed and measured some six hundred skulls from a derelict Montpellier cemetery, was another tutelary figure.[3] But there is a third individual, little acknowledged in France, whose (latent) presence is particularly striking in light of the Valéry/Rimbaud nexus Breton may have been less deluded in forging than he came to believe.[4]

In 1896, Valéry accepted an offer to move to London and commence work as a translator for the Chartered Company run by Cecil Rhodes in the lands that would eventually be named Rhodesia. In fact, he was being commissioned to furnish propaganda material on behalf of Rhodes, whose company, following a series of secret armed raids intended to topple the Kruger regime in South Africa, had become a subject of international scandal. The plan was to counteract the scandal on the continent by introducing material translated by Valéry into the French press.

Concerning this mission, two elements deserve to be underscored. First, Valéry's enthusiasm for Rhodes' colonial enterprise resonated profoundly with that phantasmagoria of potency essential to the legendary period of poetic silence. In his *Cahiers*, Rhodes would figure as one of the six living individuals he "admired personally."[5] (The others would be Poincaré, Lord Kelvin, Mallarmé, Huysmans, and Degas.) He is said to be "inebriate with pure action as one may be inebriate with pure science."[6] More strikingly, Valéry would write to Gide: "Be apprised that I am engaged in an outfit of men who are infinitely strong [*je suis dans un engrenage de gens infiniment forts*]. Thanks to my job (strictly confidential), I have learned some very important things...I woke up Tuesday facing one of the thousand pieces of a colossal machine called the Chartered Company. You have no idea of the power, the depth, the wisdom, the *brutal* clarity of these people. They are right. I am becoming aware of their *ethic*. In France, they will never be understood."[7] The accent is unmistakable. The Chartered Company, directed by Rhodes, participates in that will to mastery which brought Valéry to abjure poetry and the *sacrifizio dell'intelletto* he claimed it entailed.

There is a second curious aspect of Valéry's apprenticeship with the company. For his stay in London, the consolidation of his "poetic silence," at times felt like a trip to Africa. Again, a letter to Gide is apposite: "Ah! what a strange impression when I arrived, totally unaware of what was expected of me, anxious, and when, in my employer's residence, I was kept almost by force in a room where a Negro (*négre*) from Mashonaland served me tacitly, as I observed in astonishment the library containing books of tactics, travel, treatises on gold-mining, military manuals, etc."[8] The future -- of intellectual exaltation, poetic silence -- seemed to be leading straight to Africa. Once again, the correspondence with Gide is eloquent: "I shall perhaps be in Montpellier in a month. But who knows? I may also be in Pretoria! or in Rhodesia!"[9] The abandonment of poetry and the departure for Africa: Breton, in conflating the cases of Valéry and Rimbaud in 1914, may never have known how right he almost was.

Valéry, of course, never made it to Africa, and his silence of twenty years was relatively short-lived. That silence, however, would resonate in the poetry to which he returned. Poetry, I have shown elsewhere, returns as the tear of the Jeune Parque: a virgin awakens on a beach bedazzled and troubled by a tear: the fragment of herself now estranged from herself , she has no recollection, or understanding, of having shed.[10] Many of the poems of *Charmes* may be read as exercises, or transformations, of the "tear-work" initiated in "La Jeune Parque," an "involuntary" return to poetry that never stopped returning. As in the case of "Le Vin perdu": the poet spills a bit of red wine—as the Parque had shed her tear—into the sea without quite understanding why. In "La Crise de l'esprit," Valéry's signature essay on the state of the world after the Great War, the (no longer ex-) poet invokes the same image. The dissemination of (superior) European intelligence into areas of the world statistically more imposing, but qualitatively inferior, is compared to the diffusion of wine into water. The image, in fact, was borrowed from Henri Poincaré, one of the six individuals, including Cecil Rhodes, who was said to have earned Valéry's "admiration." For Poincaré, the image of the diffusion of wine into water was emblematic of the incontrovertibility of entropy: the wine, once dissolved, its difference obliterated, could never be reconstituted. Maxwell's demon might pretend to, but he, Poincaré and Valéry knew, had been decisively exorcised. Except, claimed Valéry, that in the domain of "the physics of the intellect," the wine might indeed be reconstituted. European intelligence, that threatened and utterly *improbable* treasure, could indeed re-emerge. The poet, having in effect pissed blood in "Le Vin perdu," becomes his own Eurologist. Or rather poetry becomes Eurology. Such is perhaps the physiological underpinning of "La Crise de l'esprit," a paean to the reconstitution of the squandered droplet: blood, tear, pomegranate seed (the "gemmes rouges de jus" of "Les Grenades") or whatever, which is, in fact, both an economic description of Valéry's poetry, in the repetitions of what I have called its "tear-work," and an affirmation of that permanence of European superiority for which he had been working under the auspices of the Chartered Company in a London that seemed to him a gateway to Africa.

But what did it mean for Valéry to *feel* European? His answer, in *Regards sur le monde actuel*, entails the evocation of two historical episodes: the Japanese incursion against (European interests in) China in 1895 and the American war with Spain in 1898. In each case, European intelligence, the treasure squandered or diffused in "La Crise de l'esprit," is turned back against Europe itself.[11] Much like the tear—- that fragment of the self that threatens the self—in "La Jeune Parque." Valéry, that is, emerges as a (threatened) European much as the Jeune Parque wakens (and awakens her creator) to poetry.

At this juncture the case of Rimbaud impinges again. For if the ground of Valéry's *poetry* is at one level the European threatened by an estrangement or diffusion of European resources turned against Europe itself, such, according to a much heralded recent biography, is precisely the horizon of Rimbaud's *silence*. The "punchline" of the epic joke of Rimbaud's career as a gun-runner for King Menelik of Choa in the Horn of Africa, according to Graham Robb, is that "Rimbaud was making a significant contribution to the first defeat of a European nation in open battle by an African army (Menelik's defeat of Italy at Adwa in 1896)."[12] To which extent, Valéry's poetry *was*, at some level, Rimbaud's silence.

But then again, Rimbaud's "silence," if we follow the provocative Robb, may not even have been his silence. Alfred Bardey, Rimbaud's associate in Aden, "had the impression that Rimbaud intended to return to literature once he had 'amassed a sufficient fortune.'"[13] There was a book on Abyssinia "that was always in abeyance," other "*beaux ouvrages*" to which he was committed. Moreover, between the numerous works he never dreamed of publishing and those other works he never, in fact, wrote, is the difference all that absolute? Might the two alleged phases of Rimbaud's career, Robb in effect asks, not be viewed as a common journey to the limit or "way of the cross," in which, the second time around," "hides and ivory" take the place of "aesthetics and Verlaine"?[14] Finally, if Rimbaud abjured "literature," was it not much as Verlaine himself had: as the repository of..."all the rest"?

Verlaine...In his search for an empirical correlate to Rimbaud's abandonment of literature, the biographer informs us flatly that Rimbaud gave up writing poems "at about the same time that he gave up living with other people."[15] It was as though poetry were a negotiation with the other, electively Verlaine. For which reason, we would look toward the one poem of Rimbaud's which was cosigned with Verlaine for enlightenment as to the abandonment of poetry. That it should bear a curious relation to the poetry of Valéry as well will, moreover, provide a secondary benefit, as welcome as it is unexpected.

"Tear-work" was our term, following a consideration of the emblematic status of the tear (*larme*) in "La Jeune Parque," for the generative agency of Valéry's poems. Curiously, the Rimbaud-Verlaine collaboration is centered on a tear-well (*larmier*) as well, but the poem "L'Idole ou le sonnet du trou du cul" is, in this case, an elegant obscenity. The asshole becomes a savage *larmier* for the secretions of the poets' (poet's?) jealous soul. The poem evokes the idyllic landscape of a human bottom in terms oddly familiar to readers of Rimbaud:

Obscur et froncé comme un oeillet violet
Il respire, humblement tapi parmi la mousse
Humide encore qui suit la fuite douce
Des fesses blanches jusqu'au coeur de son ourlet.

Familiar? Consider, after the collaborative obscenity, part of the *Album zutique*, Rimbaud's edifying "Le Dormeur du val." The evocation of an apparently sleeping soldier in a valley is couched between two holes: the "trou de verdure" or clearing at the beginning and the red bullet holes revealing, at the poem's end, that the apparently resting soldier is, in fact, dead. It is as though there were a hole-or two holes-hidden within the hole in (or of) the valley. But observe the beginning of "Le Dormeur du val":

C'est un trou de verdure où chante une rivière
Accrochant follement aux herbes des haillons
D'argent; où le soleil, de la montagne fière,
Luit: c'est un petit val qui mousse de rayons.

"L'Idole" moved toward its secret "hole" in the valley (formed by buttocks) by way of a reference to pubic "moss" (*mousse*) still moist from love. It is odd, then, that the edifying sonnet makes its way to its secret holes by way of a valley "foaming" (*qui mousse*) with daylight. Might the secret hole(s) within the hole of "Le Dormeur du val" be the very bodily orifice extolled in "L'Idole"? Or should the obscenity rather be dismissed (or admired) as a send-up of its edifying twin?

Further analysis will help us decide. Consider "Les Effarés": a group of shivering children peer in the morning's dark through an illuminated grating at a baker baking bread. As in "Le Dormeur du val," we have a cold victim (or collective victim) exposed to light and heat streaming toward them through an opening. But as in "Le Dormeur du val," there is a hole in or behind this hole. In this case, behind the grating (*soupirail*), there is the orifice (*trou clair*) of the oven into which the baker stuffs (*enfourne*) the dough of his baguette. One can imagine the *trou clair* behind the *soupirail* almost as a *trou rouge*, to use the phrase from "Le Dormeur du val." Now not only does the central act (the baker inserting his baguette into the opening) seem to resonate sexually, but the entire episode is inflected by a framing conceit. At the poem's beginning the children are evoked with their *culs en rond* or round bottoms. At the poem's end, they bend toward the spectacle with such eagerness that they split their breeches: qu'ils *crèvent leurs culottes*. This detail has been described as Dickensian (or Disneyesque), but it suffices to align this third hole (in the *culotte*) with the two others (*soupirail* and oven) to see that "Les Effarés" reenacts -- even as it answers -- our question regarding the superimposition of "Le Dormeur du val" and "L'Idole." The edifying poem about a slain soldier invites us to identify a hole within (or behind) a hole, and the superimposition of that poem with "L'Idole" supplies an obscene answer. In "Les Effarés," we are given a summation of the entire process: a hole (the oven) within a hole (*soupirail*), and behind them both a *third* hole (between *cul* and *culottes*).

Turn now to the "Lettre du voyant," the closest Rimbaud came to a manifesto, or rather to the poem included therein under the title "Le coeur supplicié." It is significantly followed by the words: "*Ça ne veut pas rien dire* [It does not mean nothing]," and is frequently interpreted as the recollection, evoked in defensively highfalutin terms, of a rape attempt on Rimbaud by a group of soldiers at about the time of the Commune.[18] The poem's first line ("Mon triste coeur bave à la poupe") has the poet's melancholy heart drooling at the stern of a ship. But the secretion at the rear recalls the *larmier*, the soul's tearwell, lodged in a different rear in the sonnet "L'Idole." Georges Izambard, the addressee of the letter, insisted on the maritime resonances of *poupe*. The poem would be an anticipation of "Le Bateau ivre," whose thrust is in part captured by two lines of "Le coeur supplicié": "O flots abracadabrantesques /Prenez mon coeur, qu'il soit sauvé." Salvation through drowning at sea is the order of the day. Moreover, Izambard notes that the maritime motif would make of the young victim less a soldier in a barracks than a cabinboy (mousse) on a ship. Once again, the word mousse recurs in our chain, but this time with a third sense: neither moss ("L'Idole") nor foam ("Le Dormeur du val"), but cabin boy. Yet once again, but with a change of gender, the *mousse* surfaces in a context of anal eroticism (*Ithyphalliques et pioupiouesques... J'aurai des sursauts stomachiques*, etc.).

Move now to the most celebrated and least *silent* (because blatantly vocalic) of Rimbaud's poems, the sonnet on "Vowels," the poem deemed in Paris to be his "masterpiece" during the years of his African travels.[19] Midst all the speculations inspired by Rimbaud's excursion into synesthesia, what seems incontrovertible is the irregular order in which the vowels are invoked: A, E, I, U, O. "O" is, of course, Omega, a fitting end to the poem, but note that the associations to U are, in fact, dominated not by the vowel, but by its near equivalent, V: "U cycles, vibrements divins des mers virides..."[20] The poem, a journey to the source, thus concludes by bringing us, idiosyncratically, from the valley of a V to the concluding orifice or hole of an O. Once again, we appear to be rehearsing the terms initiated by our superimposition of "Le Dormeur du val" and "L'Idole." And lest there be any doubt as to what the (presumably poetic) source is *of*, I would merely recall the excremental stench which lay at the beginning of Rimbaud's voyage, in the poem, to that source:

A noir corset velu des mouches éclatantes
Qui bombinent autour des puanteurs cruelles.[21]

Rimbaud's alleged "masterpiece" may indeed be a poem about bowels.[22]
All of which leads to a final speculation: that the "silence" of Rimbaud may have less to do with the will of an aspiring businessman to dissociate himself from the scandal surrounding his "literary" existence, as Robb intriguingly suggests, than with a will to move beyond a dispensation whose infantile "source," as the Freudians say, the no-longer-young genius may have intuited all too well.

1. André Breton, *Entretiens* (Paris: Gallimard, 1969), p. 24.
2. Letter to Maurice Denis in Valéry, *Oeuvres*, I (Paris: Pléiade, 1957), p. 1623.
3. Jeffrey Mehlman, "Craniometry and Criticism: Notes on a Valéryan Criss-Cross" in *Genealogies of the Text* (Cambridge: Cambridge University Press, 1995).
4. Valéry's biographer, Benoît Peeters, *Paul Valéry, une vie d'écrivain?* (Paris: Nouvelles Impressions, 1989), p. 61, refers to the episode surrounding this third figure as all the more important in that it is "so little known."
5. *Cahiers*, 1894-1914, I (Paris: C.N.R.S., 1987), p. 204.
6. *Oeuvres*, I, p.1811.
7. *Correspondence André Gide-Paul Valéry* (Paris: Gallimard, 1955), pp. 262-263.
8. Ibid., p. 263.
9. Ibid., p. 263.
10. Jeffrey Mehlman, "On Tear-Work: *l'art de Valéry*" in *Yale French Studies*, 52 (1976).
11. *Oeuvres*, II, p. 914.
12. Graham Robb, *Rimbaud* (New York: Norton, 2000), p. 381.
13. Ibid., p. 354.
14. Ibid., p. 327.
15. Ibid., p. 288.
16. Rimbaud, *Poésies complètes* (Paris: Livre de poches classique, 1998), ed. P. Brunel, p. 212. Dark and crinkled like a purple carnation, It breathes, humbly couched in the still moist moss that follows the gentle flow of the white buttocks to the heart of its rim.
17. Ibid., p. 132. It's a green opening in which a river sings, madly catching silvery shreds with blades of grass; into which the sun, from the proud mountain, glistens: a small valley afoam with daylight.
18. Ibid., p. 146.
19. Robb, p. 401.
20. *Poésies complètes*, p. 188. Eons, divine vibrations of viridian seas...
21. Ibid., p. 187. A—furry black corset of spectacular flies that thrum around the cruel stench.
22. As suggested, in conversation, by Alicia Borinsky.

Stills From 38 Seconds, 2000

A Digital Movie

Elka Krajewska

The PMA-3 is a small antipersonnel mine, which consists of a flat cylindrical body and the base-mounted UPMAH-3 chemical action pressure fuze. The PMA-3 is designed to function only when the upper pressure plate rotates within the lower assembly containing the UPMAH-3 fuze.

The emplacement directions recommend a protective cover of from 2.0 to 4.0 cm and horizontal placement of the pressure plate to take advantage of the pressure hardened or blast resistant design. Additionally, the design for a non-axial load means that the necessary pressure to function the mine decreases as the load is placed closer to the edge.

The normal pressure necessary to function the mine is described as a range of from 8.0 to 20.0 kg. However, it is possible that, when applied at the very edge, as little as 3 kg could operate the mine.

The UPMAH-3 pressure fuze with chemical friction ignitor (containing potassium chlorate, red phosphorus and binder, and glass) begins the firing train which consists of an M-17 P2 detonator containing tetryl, lead azide, and lead styphnate, and a pressed TNT main explosive charge.

The sole metallic content in the PMA-3 mine and UPMAH-3 fuze is the aluminum covering on the M-17 P2 detonator cap. This minimal metallic content does render the PMA-3 rather difficult to detect.

Due to the low operating threshold of the PMA-3, probing for this mine is very hazardous.

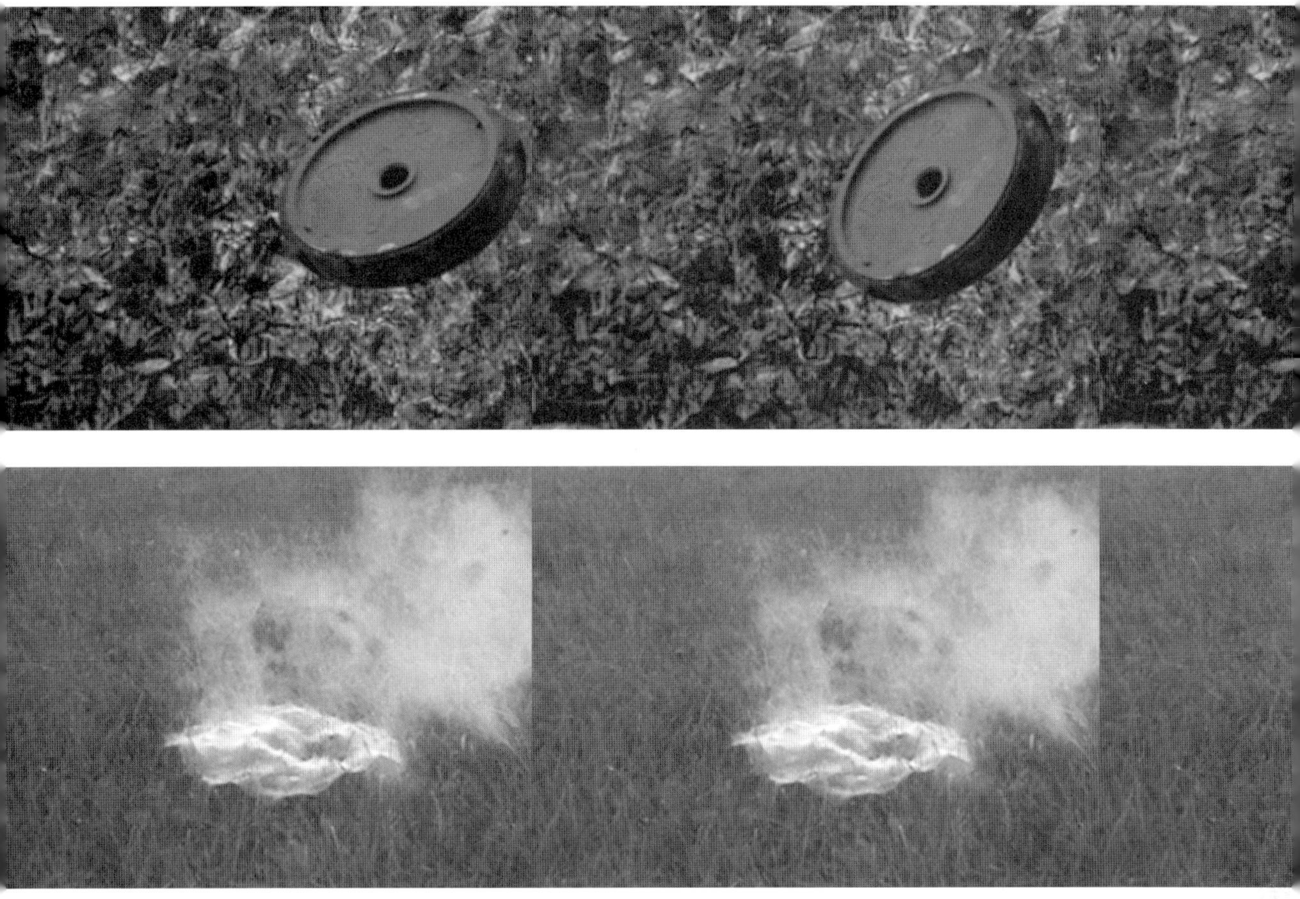

STILLS FROM 38 SECONDS 2000

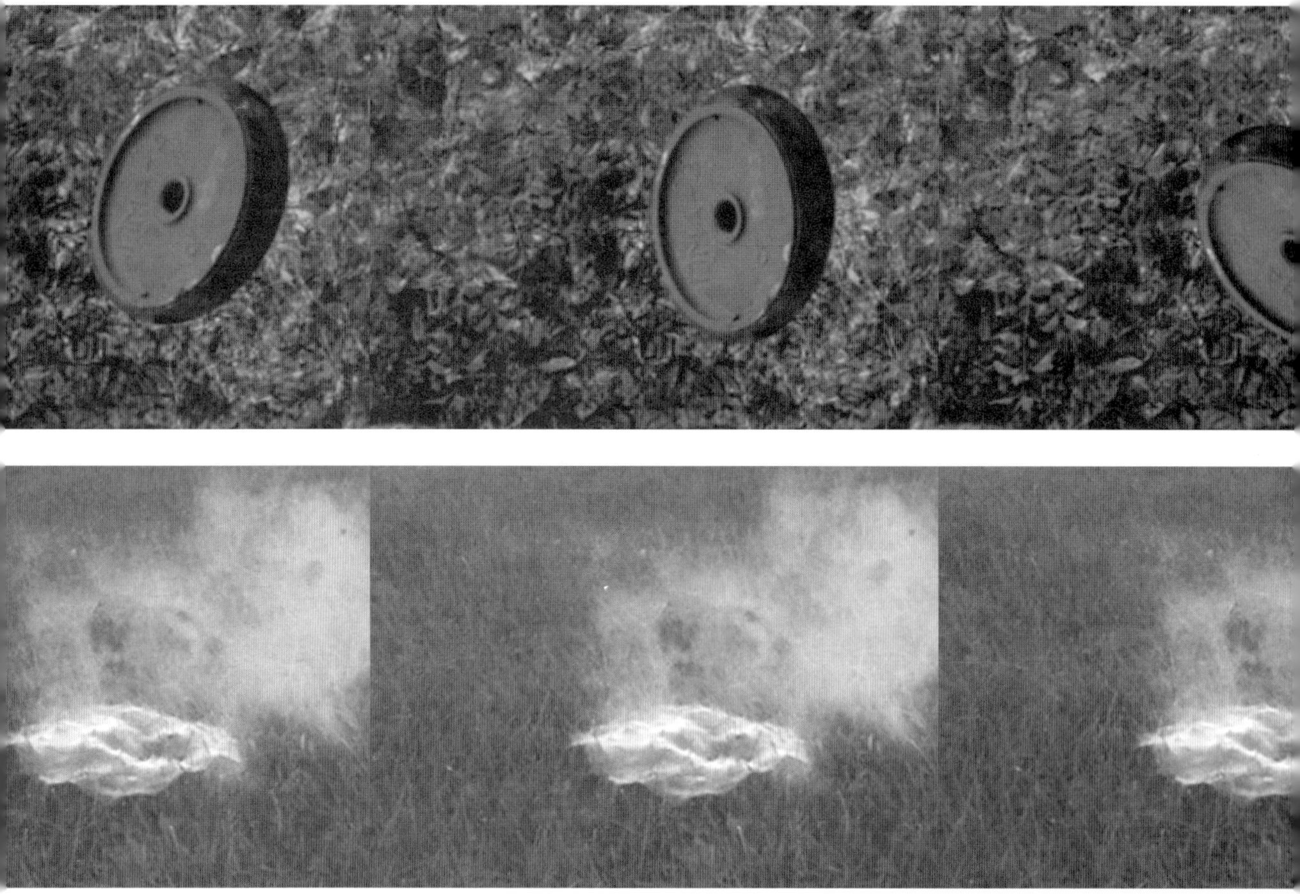

Stills From 38 Seconds 2000

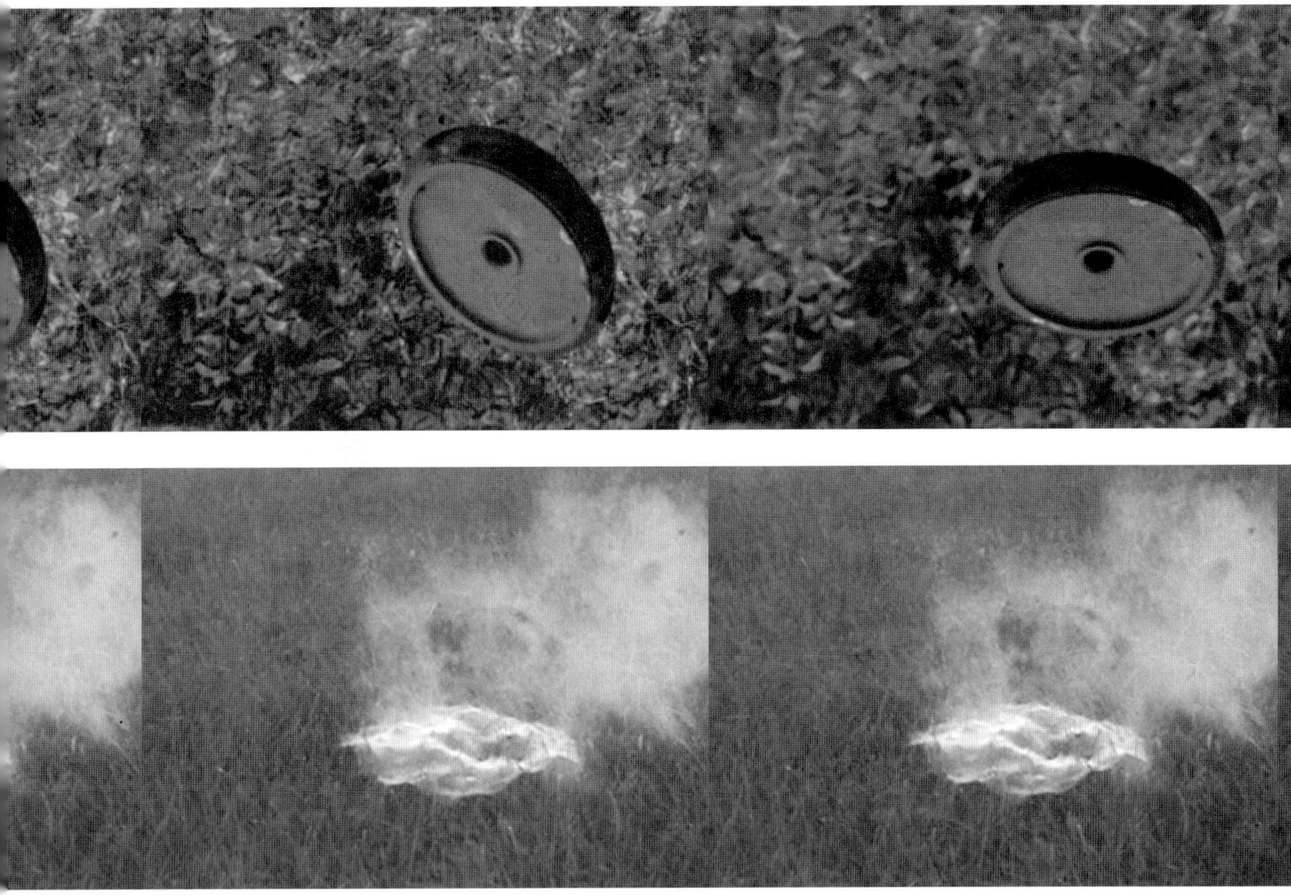

Stills From 38 Seconds 2000

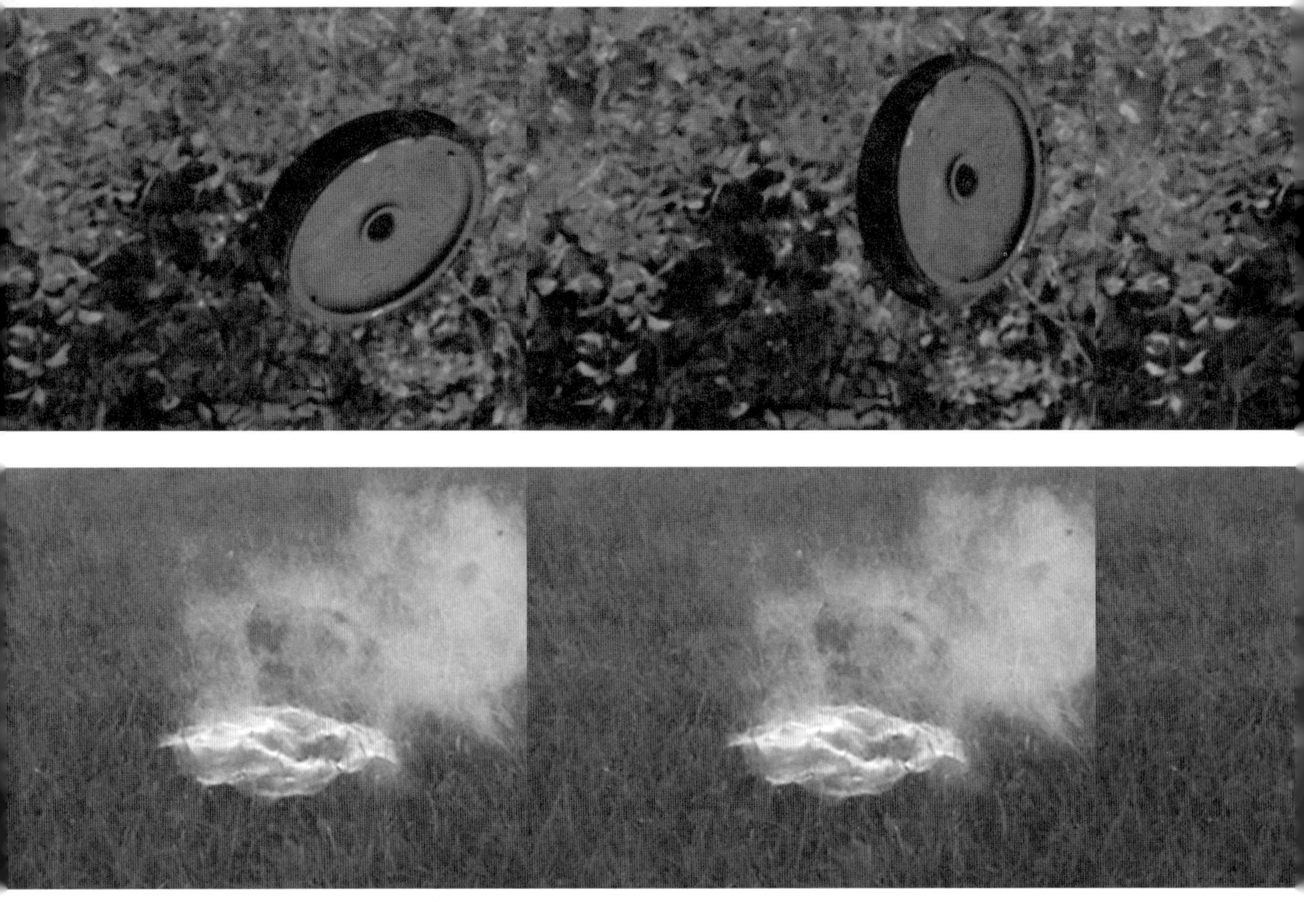

Stills from 38 Seconds 2000

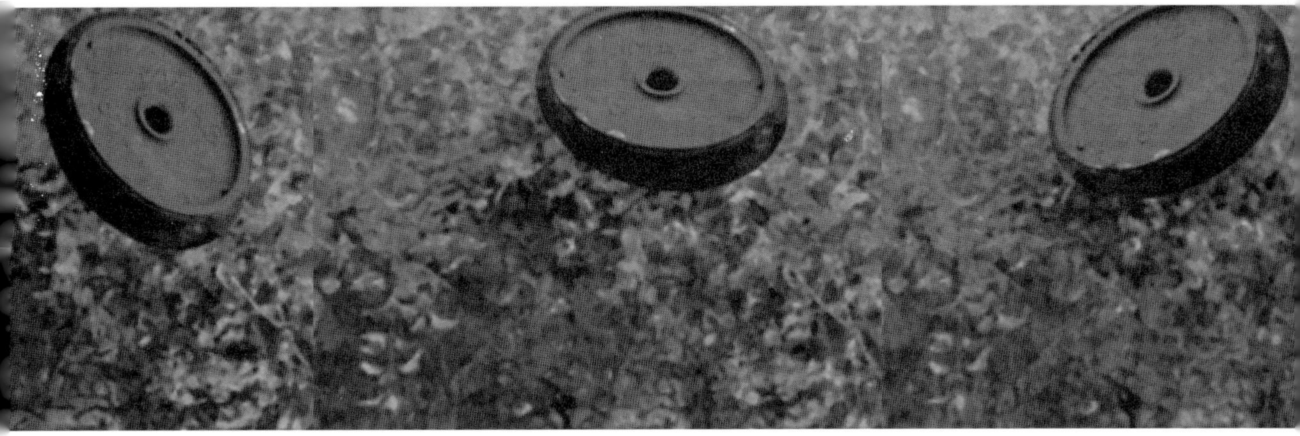

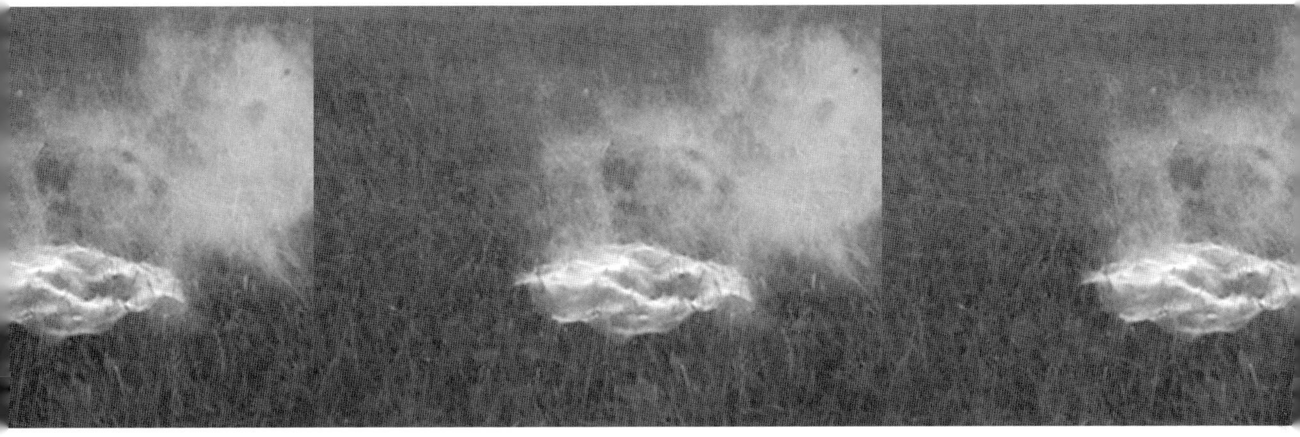

STILLS FROM 38 SECONDS 2000

SILENCE

Peter Wollen

SILENCE

When John Cage published his book *Silence*, he included a lecture he had given in Darmstadt three years previously, in 1958. Near the beginning he defined the "material" of music as consisting of "the sounds and silences" of a composition. Cage was also concerned with the "structure" of a musical composition, the division of a whole into parts, and the "method, the note-to-note procedure" adopted by the composer. According to previous methods of composition, Cage asserted, "silence was the time lapse between sounds," a device which might serve a number of purposes. It could be used to separate sounds or groups of sounds in order to differentiate them or to emphasize their relationship or to provide pauses or punctuation which would make the music more expressive. Or it could be used to give structure and definition to a musical composition. However, Cage added, "where none of these or other goals are present, silence becomes something else – *not silence at all, but sounds, the ambient sounds*. The nature of these is unpredictable and changing. These sounds (which are called silence only because they do not form part of a musical intention) may be depended upon to exist. The world teems with them and, is, in fact, at no point free of them."

Cage then went on to describe his experience in a specially constructed anechoic chamber, a room "made as silent as technologically possible" in which he nonetheless heard "two sounds, one high, one low – the high the listener's nervous system in operation, the low his blood in circulation." Or, as Cage put it in another context, "THERE IS NO SUCH THING AS SILENCE. GET THEE TO AN ANECHOIC CHAMBER AND HEAR THERE THY NERVOUS SYSTEM IN OPERATION AND HEAR THERE THY BLOOD IN CIRCULATION." In effect, "silence" became a term which denoted, for Cage, a particular type of sound, what we might call "ambient" or "environmental sound," sound which had not been deliberately created or, even if it had, had not been created as part of a musical composition, sound which had simply incorporated itself into the composition during a moment or period of "silence," a type of sound which was beyond the control of the composer. In this sense, "silence," for Cage, was akin to "chance."

Silences, Cage believed, should be loved rather than feared. Soon Cage began to experiment with "noises." As he observed, noises "had not been intellectualized; the ear could hear them directly and didn't have to go through any abstraction about them. I found that I liked noises even more than I liked intervals. I liked noises just as much as I had liked single sounds. Noises, too, had been discriminated against and being American, having been trained to be sentimental, I fought for noises. I got police permission to play sirens. The most amazing noise I ever found was that produced by means of a coil of wire attached to the pick-up arm of a phonograph and then amplified. It was shocking, really shocking and thunderous." Cage began to incorporate noise into his compositions, using chance operations to determine which noises would be used and when, willingly accepting whatever entered the acoustic field, from whatever source. Of course, in the formal context of a concert, his music was played to audiences habituated to remaining "silent."

When Jill Johnston reviewed *Silence* in *The Village Voice* in 1962, in an article entitled *There Is No Silence Now*, she observed that, as Cage conceived it, silence "means the whole world of sound, Life; and its entrance into the world of music means the end of that exclusive activity called Art whereby the composer makes a separate act meant to "illumine the darkness" of the chaos of everyday life." She continued by observing that "the admission of life into music originally meant noise" and that, by including periods of silence within his compositions, Cage was accepting "all audible phenomena as material proper for music." Cage's philosophy of music, she noted, was one that involved "his partial, sometimes total, abdication of will". This was particularly clear in Cage's silent piece, *4′ 33″*, in which no sounds are intentionally produced. The piece consists simply of the sounds made by the audience or by other chance sources within three prescribed periods of time ("movements"). As Cage himself was to put it, "the material of music, sound, is now understood not as a limited number of conventional pitches (those of the major and minor European scales) but as a field phenomenon." Music could, would and should include sounds which were, in effect, acoustic ready-mades, arbitrary sounds which had previously been dismissed as mere "noise," but which stood out against a background of supposed silence.

Yet, despite the new freedom granted to music, Cage remained quite skeptical of the value of jazz. In 1966, he began a conversation with Michael Zwerin, by explaining that: "In the first place you should know that I am very critical of jazz." He compared jazz adversely to the work of Charles Ives, who he described as suggesting "not that one thing is happening at a time, but rather that everything is happening at the same time." Cage went on to say he would prefer jazz "if we had a great deal of it at one time. Say for instance that we had twelve machines here; we could put on twelve records and immediately get a situation reminiscent of Ives, in whose music "everything is happening at the same time." Cage then announced that he preferred rock and roll to jazz. At this point, Zwerin recalled Cage's story of the "silent chamber" at Harvard and asked Cage why it was he could tolerate the loudness of rock and roll. Cage responded by noting that "silence is all of the sound we don't intend," then arguing that "therefore silence may very well include loud sounds and more and more in the twentieth century does. The sound of jet planes, of sirens, et cetera."

Cage's comments on volume reminded me of the jazz musician Sun Ra. In his book, *Space Is The Place*, John Szwed comments on the way in which jazz was first perceived as "noise" because of the layering of rhythms and the use of "unmusical effects" such as horns that imitated barnyard noises, sirens, shouts and laughter. Szwed notes that the concept of "noise" was invoked once again by those who heard Sun Ra's Solar Arkestra during the 1960s and then goes on to make a connection between Sun Ra and the Italian futurists, who used noise-creating instruments ("*intonarumor*") in response to the increasing noise of modern life. As well as special instruments and amplification, Sun Ra used force of numbers to increase noise. In 1974 he held a concert in Central Park, New York, with a hundred musicians in his Solar Arkestra – although he would have preferred ten thousand. Later that year, Zwerin described another Sun Ra performance as "total energy beyond *fortissimo*. Honking sheets of sound, grunts and screams, everybody playing as loud and fast as possible." Cage himself went to hear Sun Ra play with 100 musicians crammed into the tiny space of the Squat Theatre in New York's Chelsea. Then, in 1986, Cage performed alternately with Sun Ra at the Coney Island Museum. Noise had met silence on equal terms, so to speak, and the two proved to be commensurable.

From: Jacques Attali, *Noise*, trans. Brian Massumi, Minnesota 1985, pp 120 - 123, 'Repetition, Silence and the End of Sacrifice'.

Silence

Silence

silence **noise**

noise

silence

silence

silence

silence

silent
silence

Silence

Silencing
silence

noise

noises

noises

noises silencing
silence

silence

Noise

noise

silence
noise

noise

noise
noise

noise
noise

noise noise

noise Silences

silence

Noise

noise

noise

noise

noise

noisemaker

noise

noise

intervals

intervals

in-

tervals

intervals

SILENCE

noises

intervals **noises**

Noises

noises

noise

noises

noises

Noises

noises

noise

SILENCE

From John Cage, *Silence*, (Wesleyan, Hanover, New Hampshire), 1961, pp. 116 - 118. 'Lecture on Nothing'.

Jacques Attali's book, *Noise*, was published in 1985. Attali, who has been, in turn, a special political advisor to the President of France, the head of the European Economic Development Bank, is a prolific writer whose books include, as well as *Noise*, the fascinating study *The Labyrinth in Culture and Society*. In the beginning, music was a way of channeling noise, of subordinating the violence of noise to a formal structure, thereby providing a metaphor for society itself, as a means of governing human energies by rule. Music, at this stage, is inscribed within a communal system within which the violence of noise is tamed and ordered. Music reassures its listeners. As Attali reminds us, citing Leibnitz from *On the Radical Organization of Things*, "Great composers very often mix dissonance with harmonious chords to stimulate the hearer and to sting him, as it were, so that he becomes concerned about the outcome and is all the more pleased when everything is restored to order." Attali notes that "we find the same process in operation all the way down to jazz." In fact, even though jazz undergoes significant changes during subsequent phases in the history of music – specifically those of modification and recording – it still retains links with its origin as a social form of noise.

In the twentieth century, Attali notes, noise re-entered the system of music in new, disorderly forms – thus Russolo, one of the Italian futurists, invoked "the crashing down of metal shop blinds, slamming doors, the hubbub of crowds, the variety of din, from stations, railways, iron foundries, spinning mills, printing works, electric power stations, underground railways and the absolutely new noises of modern war." The primordial violence of noise was reaffirmed. In the wake of the futurists came Antheil with his *Ballet Mécanique*, Prokofiev with his *Pas d'Acier* and Carlos Chavez with his opera, *HP* (for Horse Power). Finally there came John Cage with an even more radical project: "When he sits motionless at the piano for four minutes and thirty-three seconds, letting the audience grow impatient and make noises, he is giving back the right to speak to people who do not want to have it." In effect, his effort to regenerate music simply appears as an act of blasphemy against music, but while he may liquidate the old, he can create nothing new.

In effect, music can never go back in time by re-creating itself as a form of ritual enacted by the composer. Cage, Attali argues, can never succeed in his radical project of leading music back again into the everyday world of noise from which it first emerged. While there has been a "fracture" in the history of music, it could only return to an original state of noise as the result of complete social breakdown, a re-winding of history back into a world of shamanism and magic. Cage's "depersonalization" of music simply leads to a form of anonymous noise, to a collapse of communication, a retrogression which can only persist as a gesture with no purchase on any possible future. For Attali the way to the future is pointed by the musicians who created "free jazz", the creators of "a new noise.. a noise of Festival and Freedom," which, so Attali hopes, "may create the conditions for a major discontinuity extending far beyond its field," introducing a truly new world of music, foreshadowing nothing less than "the emergence of a truly new society." Attali sees, in free jazz, a new kind of utopian promise.

For Attali the creation of a new "code" of noise is the necessary pre-condition for the creation of new forms of human communication and thus "the emergence of the free act, of self-transcendence, pleasure in being instead of having." As Attali conceives it, as music becomes a metaphor for society, so "free jazz" becomes a metaphor for new forms of "self-management", whose implications take us beyond music into the world of politics. Thus Attali begins to conceptualize what he calls "the new noise." First, there is music played simply for enjoyment, rather than for sale, as a concert performance or a recording. De-commercialized, music would become a form of play, with no goal beyond its own immediate production and reception. Rather than composing for audiences or consumers, musicians would play for each other, for small communal groups. As Attali puts it, "any noise, when two people decide to invest their imagination and their desire in it, becomes a potential relationship," the creation, in a nutshell, of a new social order. As Susan McClary has pointed out, Attali seems to have foreseen the appearance of garage bands, of punk or "New Wave," such as the band documented in the Colombian film, *No Futuro*, creating their own utopian world in the slums of Medellin. Or perhaps the Trinidadian steel-band playing in the Notting Hill carnival, with its escort of masquerade dancers.

Attali argues that music is nothing without noise. Modern societies, he points out, do all they can to reduce and eliminate noise, in the name of order and silence. Today, he protests, "every noise evokes an image of subversion. It is repressed, monitored. Thus the prohibition against noise in apartment buildings after a certain hour leads to the surveillance of young people, to a denunciation of the commotion that they cause." Attali describes "noise control" as an integral instrument of power by repressive state systems. Before the Industrial Revolution, he points out, "there existed no legislation for the suppression of noise and commotion. The right to make noise was a natural right, an affirmation of each individual's autonomy." Gradually a series of laws whittled away these rights – in France, article 99 of the law of April 5, 1784, followed by the law of December 22, 1789, supplemented by the ruling of November 5, 1926 (article 48), with its largely symbolic penalties. The main effort to enforce noise control came, however, in relation to the automobile – the law of 1911 prohibiting multiple horns, sirens and whistles, followed, in 1928, by the Touring Club of France's campaign in favor of noise control, followed eventually by the ordinance of February 18, 1948, limiting the use of the horn.

Attali is unsure how to judge Cage's music. He worries about Cage's apparent approval of Erik Satie's admonition that "we must bring about a music which is like furniture – a music, that is, which will be part of the noises of the environment, will take them into consideration. I think of it as melodious, softening the noises of the knives and forks, not dominating them, not imposing itself. And at the same time it would neutralize the street noises which so indiscreetly enter into the play of conversation." On the other hand, he wonders whether Cage's real intention, in thus citing Satie, might have been to open the way "for a radical renaissance" by validating ambient noise. Interpreted this way, Cage, like Attali, sought a music which would include both silence (the silence of thought rather than the silence of the oppressed) and noise: the noise of self-expression and jubilation, the irregular time, the "playing loose" advocated by Sun Ra, with his admonition, "If you can't play it perfectly right, then play it perfectly wrong." The music of incorrigibles, the sub-underground, the jesters, the "tone scientists," whose materials are not notes but sounds, each with its own timbre and volume, each with its own version of noise.

BOOKS CONSULTED AND CITED

John Cage, *Silence: Lectures and Writings*, (Wesleyan University Press, Hanover NH, 1973). First edition, 1961. Includes 'Composition As Process', lecture given at Darmstadt, Germany, in 1958 and 'The Future of Music: Credo', a talk given in Seattle in 1937, as well as 'Erik Satie', originally published in *Art News Annual*, 1958.

Jacques Attali, *Noise: The Political Economy of Music*, (University of Minnesota Press, Minneapolis MN, 1985). Translated from *Bruits: essai sur l'économiie politique de la musique*, (Presses Universitaires de France, Paris, 1977).

John F. Szwed, *Space Is The Place: The Lives and Times of Sun Ra*, (Da Capo Press, New York NY, 1998). First edition, Pantheon Books, New York NY, 1997.

Richard Kostelanetz (ed.), *John Cage, An Anthology*, (Da Capo, New York NY, 1991). First edition, 1970. Contains Jill Johnston, 'There Is No Silence Now', originally published in *The Village Voice*, November 8, 1962, and 'A Lethal Measurement', the report of a conversation between John Zwerin and John Cage, to which Zwerin added his own commentary, originally published in *The Village Voice*, January 6, 1966.

Also consulted and recommended:

Brandon LaBelle and Steve Roden (eds.), *Site of Sound: of Architecture & the Ear*, (Errant Bodies Press in association with Smart Press, Los Angeles CA and Santa Monica CA, 1999). Includes Phillip Corner, "*White Sounds Silence*", Brandon LaBelle, "*Architecture of Noise*" and David Dunn, "*Purposeful Listening in Complex States of Time.*" Also of value is the anonymous description of "*The Stalactite Organ at Luray Caverns.*"

René van Peer (ed.), *Interviews with Sound Artists*, (Het Apollohius, Einhoven, 1993). Includes Richard Lerman, "*Yes, This Is a Soda Straw, But Listen What It Can Do*", Takehisa Kosugi, "*Sound Cuisine,*" and Walter Fahndrich, *A Music of Silence*.

ONCE UPON A TIME

Ana Tiscornia

Sometime ago I tore out a picture from the *New York Times Magazine* that showed Ted Kaczynski's cabin, the unibomber's hideaway, in the middle of a huge FBI barrack. I kept it not knowing what its destiny would be nor fully knowing what attracted me to it besides the FBI's unwitting artistic set-up and, possibly, yes, an unconfessed sympathy for the character. A sympathy that didn't pretend to stand up to any analysis, not even to my own. Much later, I found myself in front of the computer manipulating that photograph in order to visualize a project: to reconstruct a replica of the cabin using a 1:1 scale but totally coated with bricks, the kind that I have often used in other works, bricks covered with a black felt imprinted with texts that are fragments of memory illness. Those photographs have now turned into *Once Upon a Time*, a work that's like a silent charge against forgetting. But this is a bit complicated because forgetfulness and silence are alike, both mark the place where what has been avoided stirs.

Silence makes possible that which is sayable; forgetfulness, repetition.

Translated from the Spanish by José Sanjinés

A Conversation with Robert Ashley

Pedro Cuperman & Owen Shapiro

Our conversation with Robert Ashley took place in his studio in the Tribeka area of Manhattan. Ashley and his wife, Mimi, who operates Lovely Music, and represents numerous avant-garde artists, occupy two massively spacious floors in an old factory converted into living quarters. One floor is Ashley's studio, sparsely furnished but fully equipped with all the electronic technology needed to compose, edit, and master his works. At the far end of the studio is a simple table with chairs and a refrigerator. Before beginning our taping Robert took from the freezer a bottle of Vodka, poured himself a small glass, straight, and offered us the choice of vodka or wine. We accepted both. The entire discussion was punctuated by short interruptions to refill glasses.

Before we continue, we must state that Robert Ashley is a composer of music and also a writer of stories. In fact, he redefined music theater/opera through his large scale works that are as much about story telling as they are about music. His librettos look to a mythic America. They are "sung" in the intoned sounds that evoke the Greek chorus. His first large scale narrative, *Perfect Lives*, was also the first television opera, commissioned by The Kitchen, in New York, in 1978, and first performed on Channel Four in England in 1984. Created as an opera for television, it was much imitated and long-revered by the cognoscenti "What about the Bible?" exclaimed with amazement John Cage, "and the Koran? It doesn't matter. We have *Perfect Lives*."

That's why it's not surprising that the first focus of our conversation was on the subject of language. The drinks didn't seem to hinder the discussion, we think.

Ashley: I think the problem for the composer who uses language is that if the language is not powerful in the sense of moving through time then you don't have very much to work with. I mean, if everything ends with "tion," in other words if instead of "to act" you have "action," then you stick with weak materials. The problem for me is always to move forward in the language; to convey ideas in the language. If I have to use "action" as opposed "to act," its harder, because action doesn't mean anything. "Action" is just a noun that describes "to act."

Cuperman: after listening to your newest opera, *Dust*, which I truly enjoyed, I wonder if your sensitivity to nouns isn't marked by your tendency to prefer narrative movements to poetry, that is, acting to metaphor.

Shapiro: Pedro is raising a question about the nature of the two angles of the artistic experience.

A: You're absolutely right, and I am reacting, strongly and personally, I am reacting to the spread of the metaphoric in our English language. I don't like it. I can understand that there was a reason for it in the 1950's, you know, with John Ashbery, who wanted to make the language more abstract, or mysterious. What has come out of that from my reading of those poems is that everything becomes metaphor. There is no direct statement at all. I mean, direct statements, there are direct statements, but they're, excuse me John Ashbery, for saying this, but whatever direct statements there are now in contemporary poetry are trivialized by this huge dependence on metaphor. I think that metaphor is worn out. I think we can't find metaphors for the most powerful things in our lives. I'm definitely reacting against metaphors. I don't like metaphors in poetry. I don't like most contemporary poetry because of this. The metaphor is not strong enough to sustain any deep feelings.

S: When you construct your narratives you still are playing with language and although you may be descriptive you end up coming up with other possible meanings for what it is you are describing. Aren't you creating metaphors yourself, not by making nouns from verbs, but from creating a series of events whose meaning is other than that which you narrate?

A: You can always interpret any act in many ways. The act has as many interpretations as there are observers to the act.

C: This is what I observed in *Dust*. Each storytelling segment seems to end in a series of repetitions which eventually creates an image charged with metaphoric value. But perhaps we are using the word metaphor in differing ways. When one listens to Philip Glass, and a series of repetitions that are apparently moving, moving, moving, in the end this movement is more then repetition, it is a mirroring event and ultimately a metaphor, perhaps in a different form then is the idea of metaphor that you may be operating by. When we use the word metaphor we also refer to that signature that allows me to call his *Beauty and the Beast* a Philip Glass and *Dust* a Robert Ashley. It can be a synecdoche but in a more radical way its the signature that condenses a whole event. I think it would be very interesting to know how you think you work, how this procedure or creative movement in music and more specifically in your compositions yields images that try to become words or rhythm.

A: It's a very difficult question because it's very difficult for me to explain what I am trying to do. All I'm saying is that the beginning of *Perfect Lives,* in the 1st or 2nd lines, I think, it says, "He takes himself seriously. Motel rooms have lost their punch for him." Now those are two absolute statements. I could have said, "they take themselves seriously." You could say that the seriousness of the situation is more important to him then the possible consequences of the next few moments. But it doesn't have enough punch. "He takes himself seriously" has more punch. There is no ambiguity.

S: But its interesting because those two statements which you call absolute statements, one direct, the other not so direct, create, like in the technique of montage, a resonance by the sheer juxtaposing of two different statements.

A: I try to make my work, my sentences, as strong as possible, with action, with verbs and with nouns that have some physical equivalent in the outside world, in the real world, in the perceptual world. For instance, "motel rooms" has a physical reality. It's not a made-up world.

C: So this means that while the story is moving forward meaning and content are diminished because of a movement continuously embedded in itself, in the telling about telling. A sort of Arabian Nights storytelling. Therefore it's either Edgar Allen Poe, trying to decipher a puzzle, or the picaresque mode, which barely leaves space for metaphor. Is that your procedure?

A: The problem that I was expressing before, in my reaction against metaphor, is that it doesn't give the listener any images that come from language.

C: Isn't that a musical bias? Sometimes poetry, like music, is also organized as a combinatory system, one note after another, not necessarily tied to meaning. Even in cases like this don't we eventually come up with a metaphor through those very combinatory procedures that you think of as "concrete"?

A: That may be true, it might be a musical bias. I don't know that. I've never thought of myself as a poet, I've always thought of myself as a storyteller. And I know that I'm a good storyteller, that I can tell a story at a drop of a hat. I can tell you a story right now. You can't tell a story in the language of contemporary American poetry. Contemporary American poetry has been robbed of the ability to tell a story. Its been stolen from contemporary America by this continual presence, this metaphor. So this idea that language should mean something else takes away all the vitality of story telling.

C: Would you say the same about Williams Carlos Williams?

A: He is one of my favorite writers. He is one of the great writers, one of my deepest influences. I've been reading *Paterson* for the past six months.

S: I was going to ask a question of a slightly different nature related to this idea of narrative. The stories are fascinating, the language very descriptive and often close to ordinary speech, but their rhythmic pattern makes it far from ordinary speech.

A: They're part of a musical construction, I would not agree that they imply metaphors.

S: I'm saying the words are metaphors, that by placing them, by altering the way that they are presented through rhythm and melody at the same time that you're telling the story, you are adding surplus information.

A: The problem for me is that I can't accept that undefined use of the word metaphor. I think that the metaphor is an accepted construction. I hate to use that word. It is intended to produce a certain effect in the reader's consciousness or imagination. I don't think that by changing the rhythms of the words, I create a metaphor. If this were to be the case everything would be a metaphor because the speaking of the language and the telling of the stories can't be separated from the voice of the speaker. So, when you read William Carlos Williams, or William Faulkner, you can't understand what's being said unless, in looking at the book, you can hear the voice of the person telling the story.

C: No matter how much action you narrate you are producing a metaphor. No matter how many metaphors you use you move me into action, into stories. It's the paradox. While I read the sad story of Kafka's Gregor Samsa my mind is progressively constructing images and totalizing an image. That's a metaphor. At the end I can't avoid producing metaphors.

S: I wonder if there's a misunderstanding; if perhaps your animosity against metaphor is because you perceive it as limiting the forward movement of musical construction.

C: What do we see, think, when we say metaphor? Is there any connection with William Carlos Williams, and you being a musician? And what about Debussy?

A: I can't answer that question because I'm not an expert on Debussy. I don't know enough to be able to speak with any authority. The important thing for the composers of my generation, I think the important contribution, especially that of American composers, has been to bring the attention of the listener back to the sound of music. I think I was always very interested in unusual sounds. Of course all composers are interested in unusual sounds. There's always a tendency in music for the idea to drift off into structural attitudes. They have to be re-interpreted. And the thing that happened in America in the last 50 years is that David Tudor and John Cage focused on the perceptual enjoyment of the sound, to focus people's attention on the sound as an object, as in Morton Feldman, Alvin Lucier, and so many other composers. The emphasis has been to make people pay attention to the sound, and of course sound occupies time, and evokes some kind of consciousness to what many people call meditation. That's just one appreciation of music. The idea that you listen to the sound of something is a radical difference from the idea of listening to the arrangement of sounds. To listen to the sound is one thing, to listen to the arrangement of the sound of music as the composer constructs it is a different idea. Therefore the ideal is to just listen to the sound, you just appreciate the sound, as in sex.

S: Is it a question of focus or emphasis to you? Or is it that before Cage and Tudor the focus was not on sound but on the composition, so much so that sound was silenced?

A: Yeah, the sound wasn't important. Before the 1950s, music had drifted into an idea that the arrangement of the sounds was the essential thing. If you didn't understand the arrangement of the sound then you didn't understand the music. What has happened in the last 50 years is that the principle was to make people focus on the sounds, like they would focus on any one of the other sensual experiences. Then the composer has to figure out arrangements of the sound that don't distract the listener from the absolute sound, but keep the listener focused on the sound itself. This is what composition is for me.

S: So, you're responding to Schoenberg and other such composers who have created systems?

A: Yeah, I don't think that it's not interesting to me. I like Milton Babbit's music because the restrictions that he imposed on himself to make the arrangement of the sound fit some sort of pattern that actually produced some original sounds. We also have to give Babbit credit for his interest in new kinds of sounds, electronic sounds. Its not the same like the simple propositions that David Tudor makes out of this day and age. You give up to this sensuality of the sound. You surrender to that sensuality.

S: So it is sex?

A: Yeah, sort of. It's like sex, but there's nothing like sex.

S: The way one would mark sound might have something to do with silence?

C: I sensed in what you are saying that there is perhaps a sort of composition, a sort of strategy in which metaphor participates. You use the word sex, which implies a kind of duration. Would it be an oversimplification to say that sound, like sex, is patterened around duration? I am not a musician, but I wonder.

A: There's no answer. I don't think that anybody can appreciate the mind of a musician. The reason you become a musician is because of the thrill that you feel in the sound. You don't decide to be a musician because the combinations make a lot of sense to you or because you're interested in very complicated ideas. You decide to become a musician because the thrill of the sounds is so powerful that it captures you. You don't know what the structure is. You don't know what the meaning is. All you know is that the sound devastates you and it takes you out from where you are and puts you somewhere else. That condition is what you try to recapture for the rest of your life. Literature is different. I can't honestly speak of the intellectual experience of literature, I mean I read a lot, because I don't have the desire to be a writer like William Faulkner, Borges, etc. I don't know what that desire is. I'd rather be a baseball player. I've never wanted to be a writer. I've always wanted to be a musician because of that voluptuousness of the sound I experienced when I was a child, and I won't give up trying to find it. Do you understand me?

C: But, in saying that, you are kind of an old fashioned medieval storyteller.

A: It's incidental to who I am. Alvin Lucier doesn't tell stories and his music is beautiful.

S: Aren't you describing the relationship between the artist and his medium?

A: You became a filmmaker because when you see film it changes you, and that change feels good. That sensuous aspect is absolutely undeniable. In Western European tradition, from the late Middle Ages, there was increasingly the idea that you started from someplace, you introduced different musical characters and you treated those characters in a way that was dramatic, in a narrative sense, then you resolve that drama at the end of the piece. It makes it a kind of musical narrative, a story. The music of Beethoven, the father of modern music, makes a story. I think that before him, that might have not been true. I think that there could have been other reasons for music that were not narrative reasons, and I know that in music of other cultures today there is not necessarily the idea of a music narrative, so we are discussing something that is extremely Eurocentric. I'm European; I'm not ashamed of my culture. European music has only a five hundred year history.

S: When composers take ideas from other world music, like Chinese music, are they borrowing just the sounds or are they using these sounds to serve narrative functions?

A: One's experience with Chinese opera, or African drumming, or Arabic string playing is totally sensuous, you don't even care about the structure. You just listen to it because the sound is so compelling. You're drawn to the sound the same way a bug is drawn to the light. Finally, if you are a smart bug, you can figure out what light is all about, what people think of the light. The composer's job is to trick you into listening. If you're composing, say for 3 minutes, your job is to keep people listening. If you're composing an opera you're job is to keep people listening for 3 hours. To keep people listening you have to keep the sensual experience of the sound.

S: Do you think this is the case of John Cage's "*4:33*" (where, paradoxically a pianist sits at the piano without playing a note for 4:33 minutes)?

A: "*4:33*" is a kind of theoretical milestone in that it forces the listener to become aware of sounds that otherwise would be excluded. We know from our experience and from science that listening is very selective. We could be playing music now and talking at the same time and I'd be listening to what you're saying as opposed to listening to the music. The selectiveness of listening was a scientific discovery on the same day that John Cage wrote *4:33*. What John did was not to validate science in any way. It was just another expression of that understanding of what you're paying attention to is what the music is. John made people pay attention to something they never paid attention to before. He made music out of a compositional decision. He didn't change the rules of selective listening he just changes what you are listening to. He just changed the game.

1st Interlude

Ashley took a break leaving Cuperman and Shapiro alone in the studio to reflect on the conversation and sip their drinks. Ashley returned and poured himself some more vodka. The conversation continues.

A: When I was working on this piece that had to do with Cuban Spanish, and coincidentally I read an article in the *New York Times Literary Supplement* that was describing the whole issue of translations. It said that in South American Spanish you can have different tenses of the verb in the same sentence, you can have past, present, and future all in the same sentence, and that's impossible in English. In translating from the Magical Realist Spanish writers to English you would have to make choices of tenses. You have to break down the sentence and you're losing themagic of the meaning. If you can translate the past, present and future in a sentence obviously it's magic. But if you have to break the sentence out you lose the magic.

C: Its more than the verb, its more than the point-of-view. I think Faulkner could aslo do this, perhpas because he read very carefully seventeenth-century Baroque authors.

A: Faulkner doesn't give you any clues. He writes in a consistent verb tense, without ever giving you any indication of how those different tenses fit together, and the English is perfect. It is magic in that you never know where you are in time.

C: But you always sense the presence of the present telling voice, of the vocalizing voice. You never lose touch with the present voice. This is what is more interesting then the shift in time, through shifts in tense the shift in point-of-view. One has the sense that there is a game being played between time and voice. It is very interesting that you should admire that which is structural, compositional, because the magic is there.

A: People say to me that in my work, they don't know what time it is. It jumps from one time to another time without any markings. I consider that to be a compliment and I learned that from William Faulkner. I've been re-reading a collection of short stories, but they're not just a collection of short stories. They all have the same people in them. They are a collection of people from different generations, but when you first start reading the stories there's a character in there that you don't even know is a human being until you get 30 pages in. There is this complicated story in which this person goes to another plantation. It is about this girl and a guy who has a poker game and has to get the girl back home. Then the next chapter of the book is about the grandmother of this guy who was a floating character in the first story. You read the book and you can't figure out what the time is.

S: But you also do point-of-view shifts. Its not just the idea of tense differences, of who the teller is in time but also who the character is literally.

A: That's easy to do when you have different voices. When you have the actual physical voice telling the story, the person of that voice takes you in; you accept all the conditions of that person telling the story. And then when the voice changes, you have another set of conditions.

C: When you say "you," who do you mean?

A: The listener.

C: The listener or the storyteller?

A: Both.

C: Because when I was listening to you, there was a you, and there was an I, and an incarnation of another voice, and then there were shifting voices. Then a regression to the original.

A: Well, right now I'm speaking the way I speak to everybody. I can change that in a moment and I can become a politician. Its easy to do that, and its especially easy to do that in music composition because when the composer changes the performer's voice, for one thing you have a whole new set of conditions because the performer's voice is a different person/character. "OK Jackie, you sing in A flat. Tom, here's a B flat. Tell me the story in B flat." He can't be anything but the character in B flat.

C: So characters have no personality?

S: It's your code.

A: It's a code. All actors know this. Even if you're not using musical phrasing techniques, the composer is going back to one of the most basic elements of our understanding of character. I could never be a presidential character, a politician, with my voice. I would have to change my voice to become a politician.

C: If there were a change in character, how would this shift be changed in musical terms? Would there be a change in pitch? Is there a pitch narrative?

A: When we start working on a piece, if I give a singer a certain pitch which is almost at the top of her musical range, she has to negotiate all the musical items to stay on that pitch. If I give another pitch, which is at the bottom of her musical range she becomes a different character.

S: Do you think about the use of an opposition? If that character wants to be serious, would you lower the pitch? Or change the construction of the words?

A: You would lower the pitch. You would probably also change the construction of the words, but definitely lower the pitch. Your pitch expresses a certain character, of earnestness, or seriousness, urgency, whatever. When I ask a singer to sing at a different pitch, I rarely write out the melodies. I give the singer the pitch and say "tell me the story and break my heart."

C: So this is the closest you will get to poetry?

A: Poets are such bad readers, universally disappointing.

S: Would you ever change the character using the same singer. In other words would you ever have a given singer play the part of more then one character or would you switch to another singer with another pitch?

A: You'd change the singer. Every singer has a range about an octave or octave and a half. If I take Joan La Barbara, her top pitch is A flat over middle C. If I ask her to sing on that A flat she doesn't have anywhere to go above it. She has a long way to go below it. So, that determines the character of who she is. On the other hand she has a low E flat which is an octave and a half below that A flat over C. If I ask her to go sing at E flat she hasn't anywhere to go below that but a long way to go above it. So, it changes her character by what is available to her, it is the technique of telling the story at that pitch. All singers have specific ranges. They don't have anywhere to go beyond that range. I give them a pitch because we have an agreement that they will sing their character on that pitch but you can do anything you want within it, to make stresses, accents, anything that helps express the emotion of the music.

S: You have a character that is singing an A flat above middle C, and you want them to tell their story at that pitch, then you have another character who is at a higher pitch, would you ever shift the character while the story the first singer tells continues, and is picked up by the next singer?

A: In the latter pieces, in a quartet of the operas, *El Aficionado, Improvement, Foreign Experiences, Now Eleanor's Idea*, the quartet uses the most dramatic examples of changing the pitch for the singer so the singer produces a different character. So the character is established by the pitch. For example, if Jackie (Jacqueline Humbert) is singing a D flat, above middle C, which is exactly in the middle of her range and her most beautiful sound, if her chord changes, like to a C minor chord, her character doesn't change. She is well within her range from the D flat. But if she goes up to an A flat above the D flat, which is really out of her range, she becomes a different character.

C: The story changes. This is the problem with a combinatory system. Can one story be consistent with another and still be the same? In literature this can happen.

S: And that can be literalized by the use of different performers. So, if you have a performer whose pitch height is A flat but the story the performer is being told to tell is above that, then the story gets taken over by another singer whose pitch is at that level. So, what is happening, narratively, is you have a continuous story, but it is shared by two different performers. In which case the character is literally transformed into another character.

A: I don't use that technique.

S: I'm thinking of something more directly related to your musical construction. Do you know Luis Buñuel's *The Obscure Object of Desire?* There are two different actresses who don't look anything alike but who play the same role. The male character never responds to their shifting as if there's anything wrong, or strange. So, the audience is watching a male character and they're in the bedroom and the one actress excuses herself and when she returns it's the other actress. Everything continues as if nothing happened. The male character responds as if it's the same person. In fact, the audience doesn't see two different actresses.

C: Because the "pitch" is the same. They incarnate the same semantic definition. It was an accident. Even though they are two different people the fact that they play the same psychological combinatory role makes them equal no matter how their faces change. Here we have two roles that are the same played by two different persons, but we don't perceive it.

S: I'm just asking if there's a musical analogy to that. When I think about *El Aficionado* there is a lot of shifting that goes along with the narrative throughline. Sometimes I'd feel one character is continuing the story that another was on but I recognize it was two different characters. It's a plot line. That's why I asked the question. The shifting of pitch is really fascinating.

A: The idea of what pitch your speaking of is so profound; its such a powerful tool in composition that I resort to it. It's the basis of my work in establishing characters. In Improvement Jackie sings on four, five, six different pitches in different scenes. She's a different character in different scenes. So if you're a fan of Peter Sellers, he loved to shift characters, he shifted the pitch of his voice. The British are actually better at that than Americans because of the caste system. They have a specific idea of how you sound if you're in a different caste.

C: So, we could say that "in the beginning there was not the word, there was the pitch."

A: In the beginning it was the pitch. Silence, as a label, is definitely John Cage's territory. You have to give him credit for putting a label on that territory. But in fact in musical composition you can, the composer can, admire and love John Cage's music, but at the same time one can put aside his theoretical definition of silence. In music you can create silence by leading the listener to listen only to certain kinds of sounds. You can have the sound element stopped for a moment, ten minutes, whatever, you can create a more or less absolute silence in the perception of the listener because the listener is only looking for a certain kind of sound. If the listener doesn't hear that sound, the listener hears absolute silence. There can be longer pauses in music where attention is distracted by the traffic, and John would say that's part of the idea. The composer can train the listener to listen for just one kind of sound. All other kinds of sound one excludes from the realm of sound. You can train the listener to have the experience of absolute silence from a scientific point-of-view it's an illusion but it's a valid illusion from a composer's point-of-view. Right now I'm talking in between the sounds that I'm making, you are excluding all else. I can train you not to hear those sounds.

2nd Interlude

At this point in the conversation the phone rang. Like a character in one of his operas Ashley offered Cuperman some more vodka, and Shapiro some more red wine as he poured himself another glass of vodka while speaking on the phone. When he returned the subject shifts to *Dust*, his most recent opera.

A: It's about people who are in the margins of society because they are poor, old, have mental problems. It's a sort of obvious narrative. When they play these songs in the hospital (the opera's final scene takes place in a hospital room) they are different from his memories. The memories have a certain color in the process.

S: When you shift the pitch it makes the song speak to the idea of memory. What do you title the song in the end?

A: In the end is called the "Angel of Loneliness." It has some silences, which bring it to a close. The longer the silences the more the piece slows down until it stops with "There's nothing wrong with you. (repeated several times, each repetition occuring between increasingly long pauses before the last line, "That a little love can't fix," is allowed to end the opera).

C: While I was waiting for the next sound I was about to witness the metaphor of death. The sound wouldn't come.

A: The piece is going full blast for an hour and a half and you just have to figure a way to stop it.

S: You can stop the piece by stopping?

A: I couldn't have them say, "there's something wrong with you that a little love can't fix." The piece is not over. It has been going for 90 minutes. You have to figure out some way to slow it down and actually make it stop. You have to figure out some way to make it stop so that the old man says the last word. That's the end.

S: But isn't that drawing on existing codes that signify "the end"? Like in a Beethoven symphony, you get the final notes which bring it to an end. It's a classical code.

C: When one listens to the last song the narrator's voice is like radio stories. The voice creates the images, generating new kinds of attitudes toward perception. I was waiting for the sound. Silence. So there is such a thing as 'waiting for the expected sound.'

A: As long as you pay personal attention to the sound and the sound is changing things for you then I have succeeded. If the sound starts slowing down then you start expecting the end, then when the end comes it seems right that I have succeeded. The silence makes the piece stop.

C: So, the end is the end of the story and of the music and it becomes very powerful. When the last note occurs you could expect that it could continue and not be the last note. That's what creates the powerful notion of death. There's no way of representing death because we don't know what it is.

A: "One more time" refers to this guy who is a very old man. He doesn't want a girlfriend, he just wants the experience of falling in love one more time. Because when you fall in love time stops. When you fall in love everything is in the future. Now this guy is getting old so he doesn't have a future anymore. So he wants to fall in love one more time so he can have that experience of the future.

C: It's not just a narcissistic thing; he wants to give pleasure to somebody else.

A: That's part of falling in love.

C: I sense a lot of irony in the piece. Especially in the way you treat the theme of age?

A: I'm sure there's that. I can't help it. Popular music has a different role for us because it's designed to remind you of something you already know. Popular music has a powerful element of nostalgia. Where what I'm working with, what Phil (Philip Glass) is working with, there's nothing I can remind you of because we haven't experienced it except as a nostalgia for 30-50 years ago. There was a great excitement about the power of music, especially in Europe after the war. This enormous excitement was about the relationship between new music and progress, change, something like that. So, what everybody is working on or working from is a nostalgia for that time where the future seemed to be more interesting then the present. I think that all of us, even the youngest composers, have lost that vision that music is connected to social change and so the music is less attached to a social vision. We are more arbitrary about where you are in musical history and that is the difference between what's happening today and what happened 30-40 years ago. I think the war (Vietnam) is a real factor for that consciousness. After the war people were very hopeful about the idea of big social change, but for some reason the music was very involved in that. 1960s music represented the possibility of a profound social change and that did not happen and so music was kind of discarded as an omen of the future. I think now composers are more involved in their own personal histories because they're trying to understand those histories more than trying to understand the relationship of music to politics and social change. Now everyone is demoralized.

S: I feel that too. I was just wondering if that has to do with the notion that Americans are a-historical.

C: That is the problem.

S: We're ethnocentric, chronocentric and geocentric. We're not connected to any kind of history. Our history is of the moment, and somehow we've exported this sensibility to the rest of the world as well. Given the technological age that we live in and the need for instantaneous gratification, we just don't seem to have any connection to a history.

A: I mean it's true that America is very special and that we're so young and so naïve. I mean we have no history for all practical purposes but that just makes us more vulnerable to the technological, to the changes that technology produces. It produces a society, it makes us seem like we're causing it, but I don't think we're causing it, I just think that we are more vulnerable. Since we have no history we are extremely fragile in our relationship to technological changes. I don't think it's a matter of the world being more Americanized, but it is being only colonized by technology and we just happen to be the easiest victims because we have no historical protection or perspective. See, the thing is that I like technology and I think that it's true that technology has made us more secular. It's taken away religion. Maybe it is a religion. I'm not so interested in the idea of a fascination with death. If you're a totally secular person then the end of life is just that, the end of life, and there's no big deal. We are definitely going into something that's remarkable, and its going into something in the last five hundred or a thousand years of European history. From a secular point-of-view you're either alive or you're dead. If you are dead you're not here and it doesn't matter. So you don't think about death as another aspect of life, you just think about death as being nothing, you have gone and so you've changed the whole idea. By getting rid of your idea of death you've changed your whole idea of life. You've just eliminated a huge burden on life by getting rid of death.

C: "One more time" is that a Jewish phrase or an oriental phrase when you say "one more time"? Is it reincarnation or is it bye bye?

Ashley: No, no, no, it's not reincarnation, it's bye bye.

Nam June Paik

Five Screens

A Trip to Nam

Izhar Patkin

Sometime in the late 80's of the last century, on the occasion of a Whitney Museum Biennial we both participated in, Nam June Paik asked me if I would make some collaborative works with him. This was quite an amazing proposition for someone who, as a teenager, first encountered Paik's work on a trip from Israel to the Stedelijk Museum in Amsterdam. I remember, in all my enthusiastic teen authority, declaring that Paik's way was the way! It was a sculpture of God watching TV. Watching himself on TV (a hip Italian TV in white plastic).

Twenty years later, I am having lunch with Nam to discuss our collaborative project but before we get to our business he has a burning question for me.

"Tell me about your God"

- My God?

- Well yes, the Bible.

- Why?

- I have to do a piece with a biblical theme for a show in Europe, I have never read the Bible and they never taught it in school. I found it so reassuring that he didn't know the stories of the Bible. I didn't have to pretend that I knew more about Buddha than I actually did. In Hebrew we say, what a "luxus" (luxury)! Now he would make a biblical sculpture based on my recollections of the Bible and all of Europe would stand still in front of his moving images and project their stories onto it. How very Fluxus!

We started our collaborative sculptures. We introduced our Gods to each other and we sent them on a highway ride without maps of the Diaspora or any other destinations that ex-patriots often make pilgrimage to. What freedom!

Nam was complaining about foot pain.

- Are you Ok?

- Well, sort of. It is to be expected, the Buddha is punishing me for all I have been doing to him.

- What about me? Are you trying to rope me into a Buddhist hall of punishment now? Jews have enough troubles of their own.

- Don't worry! The Buddha can only torture a Buddhist.

MR. PAIK, WHY DID YOU EAT THE PIANO?

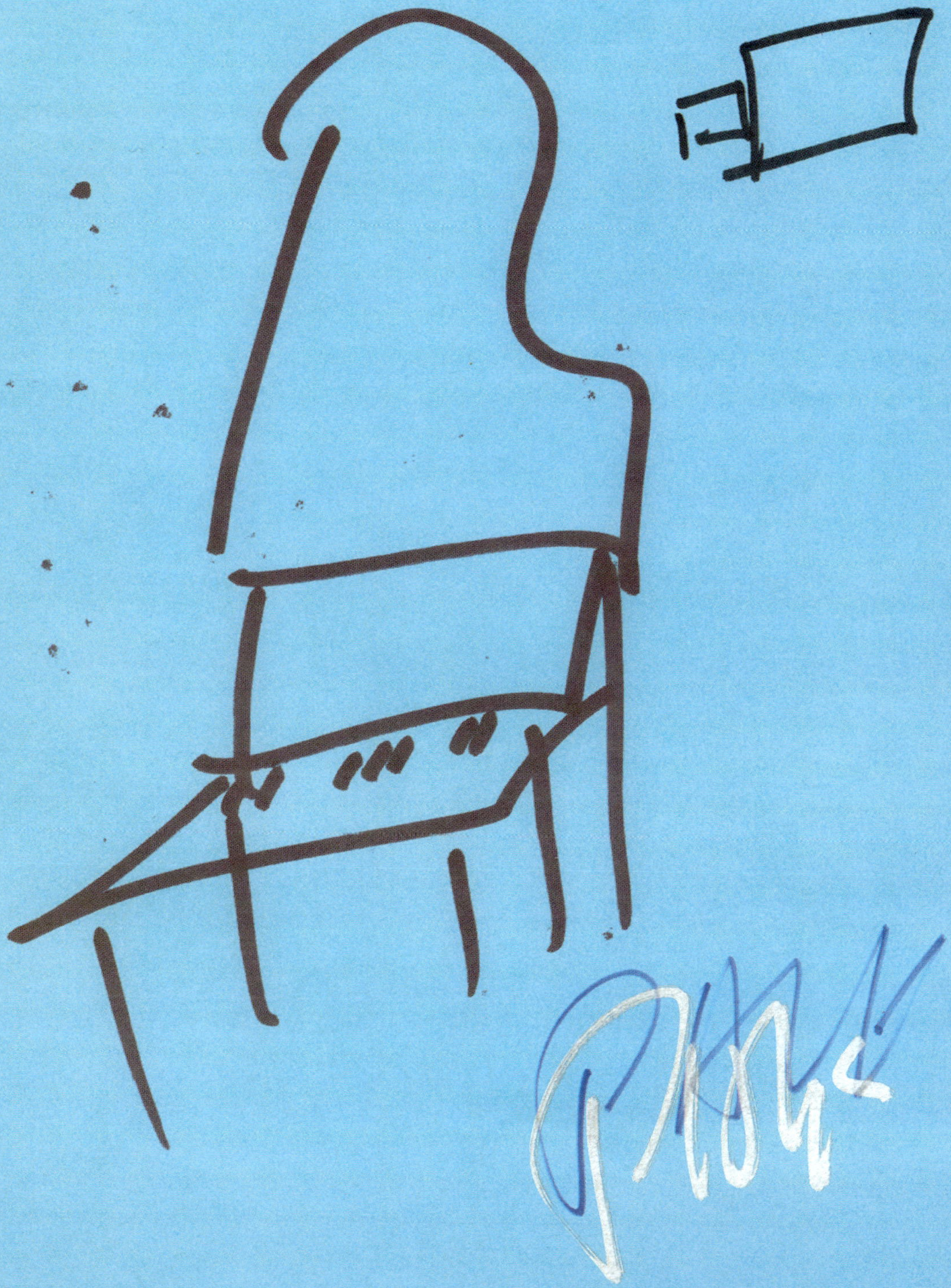

MR. PAIK, WHY DID YOU EAT THE PIANO?

because
I was
Hungary.

2000

MR. PAIK, WHY DID YOU EAT THE PIANO?

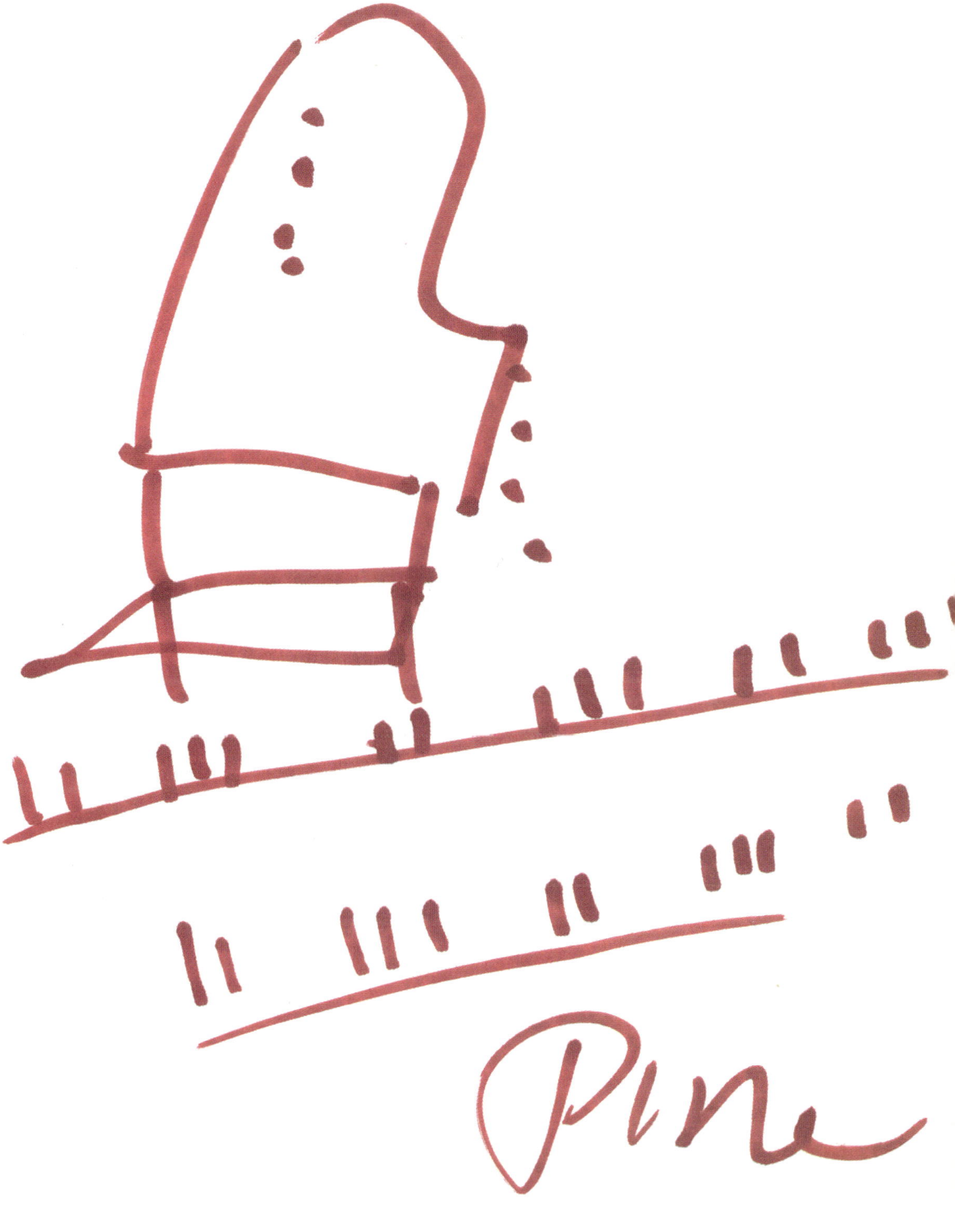

MR. PAIK, WHY DID YOU EAT THE PIANO?

Because

I was

HORNY.

Paik

2.000

7/9

Because

John

Cage

made

silence

famous

WHITHER
SILENCE?
WITHERS...

Andrew Waggoner

The colonization of silence is complete. Its progress was so gradual that even those who watched it with alarm have only now begun to take stock of the losses. Reflection, discernment, a sustainable sense of tranquility, of knowing where and how to find oneself, these are only the most obvious casualties of ubiquitous Sonus's march to the sea. Much more insidious has been the loss of music itself.

But this can't be: Music is everywhere; we have more of it, available in more forms, more often, than at any time in human history. I can go to the web and find, *O King of Berio Why Are We Born* (not to have a good time) of the young Buck Owens, Pat Boone's version of Tutti Frutti; I can find all the same at the mall. Surely this is a good thing. I can find renewal of spirit in *Sur Incises* of Boulez, or ponder the hoary depths of human idiocy in Schmidt's *Book of the Seven Seals*. Music is everywhere. Long live it.

Just give me five minutes without it; that's all I ask, perhaps all I'll need to bring it back into being for myself. Imprisoned by it as I am now, assaulted in every store, elevator, voice-mail system, passing car, neighbor's home, by it and its consequent immolation in the noise of the quotidian, it is lost to me as anything other than a kind of psychic rape. When music is everywhere it is nowhere; when everything is music nothing is.

Silence is as crucial to the musical experience as any of its sounding parameters, and not merely as a kind of acoustical "negative space." Silence births, nurtures and eventually takes back the musical utterance; it shapes both the formation of its textures and the arc of its progress through time.

And, of course, since silence—unless one is in an anechoic chamber—is never wholly silent, its presence, its expression allows us to distinguish between sounds that are and are not music. Thus is not-music given entry into music. Cage aside, the sounds in the hall, in the street, in the club, are not music, though they become part of the shared discourse that is; they are the fragments of conversation overheard but uncomprehended by speakers of a different language, passionately engaged in their own dialogue amidst the whirl of an alien culture. Thus is music's wonderful strangeness amplified by a silence that is always trying to tell us something. Exactly what it tells us can be very precise, at least in musical terms. A few examples:

The spaces that enfold the last phrases of Webern's *Three Orchestral Songs of 1913-*

14 open a door for us into an understanding of "O neige Dich, O komme wieder, Du grüst und segnest—Der Hauch des Abends nimmt das Licht-Ich seh's nicht mehr, Dein liebes Angesicht" (Oh bend thyself, oh come again. You breathe and bless. The evening breeze whisks away the light; I don't see it anymore, your dear face...) that most of us cannot access through a reading of the text alone. We are drawn into a time-sense that seems to emanate from a quantum glacier: things seem both very big and very small (perhaps the elusive grand unified theory of physics lurks somewhere in Webern's music). Thus, with the solo whispering of "Du grüst und segnest" the surrounding silence amplifies the softness of Du, the sibilance of segnest; the intimacy of this direct entreaty to what for Webern amounted to a ground-of-being is made almost overpowering, embarrassing even, by the variegated acoustical richness of each syllable. "You greet and bless" becomes a sacred utterance of hushed sensuality that transforms the "soft mountain radiance," the "Mother of grace" whose "dear face [we] see no more" into a departed lover. It is neither the words themselves, nor the fact that they are whispered, nor even the the sparseness of the pianissimo accompaniment with which they overlap that endow them with such heady signification. It is their purposeful wading into aural nothingness that makes them so special, so haunting, so naked.

In Webern's *Variations* op. 30 something similar happens, though here the affective experience is not text-dependent. At the work's outset individual attacks are set off from each other by the silences that separate them. Our sense of the attacks, their lengths and intensities, is determined by the lengths of the silences. As we move through the piece and individual attacks are layered with others of varying durations, finally yielding extended lines, our apprehension of shape is fueled by the recollection of past silences in our present, echoic memory; we continue to experience silence through the welter of polyphony, a silence of many levels and relative intensities of soundlessness. This form-giving potentiality of silence, that is to say the active memory of silence as an agent in the musical discourse, is so important in Webern's music as to be generalized as a natural force.

This is a basic feature of much other music as well, of course, really of all musics on some level. What was a tacit understanding for most composers before Webern, however, became for him a central expressive principle. Thus can we say that without a silence within which to develop, and with which the listener is well-acquainted and comfortable, Webern's music only half-exists at best.

The same can be said of Morton Feldman, in whose late works a different — but no less dynamic — sense of silence is at play. In For Samuel Beckett, to take just one example, a massive texture unfolds slowly, almost imperceptibly, with columns of sound fanning out inch by sonic inch, their relationships to each other constantly changing through a gradual process of temporal displacement. The effect at first could be described as prismatic (analogy fails us, but it's all we have), with shafts of light intermittently piercing the slow turning of these huge shapes. Further on, however, it begins to feel as if the texture is breathing, with dynamic swells resulting naturally from the juxtaposition of different timbres. Listen further still and we now find silences parting the texture and defining the large-scale motion of the piece. In constructive terms they are the result of the ever-widening spaces created by the successive augmentation of the textural canon that runs from beginning to end. The affective sense, however, is just the opposite: it is silence that is the work's pulmonary engine; silence asserts itself with greater and greater confidence, with a stronger sense of self, until it clears away the texture and is left with only itself, only its own perfect wholeness. Not to be crass, but the piece can feel as if it's all about the business of silence clearing its throat. Certainly for those who love Feldman's music and are able to stay with it to the end the effect is tonic, serving to endow one's own cluttered life with a sense of space.

What do Webern's and Feldman's aesthetics tell us about our lives, our time? How do we locate them within a century of clanging metal and noisy data? For Webern it may have been the composing-out of a singular view of art as the willful emanation of nature, the incarnation in pure, formal sentience of the structural purity of the cosmos. Feldman's view was equally rich and evocative, though expressed in more workaday terms (he once remarked that like a tailor, he was a craftsman; "the suit fits better" he said). On a personal level one could conclude that Webern, a small, seemingly quiet and introspective man was born to write small, quiet music. How then to explain Feldman? Big, garrulous, fun, brilliant, obscene, he seemed to present a persona that defied connection with his music.

This kind of second-guessing is nonsense, of course (though it's fun). There is absolutely no way we can know the psychic path of anything as complex as an aesthetic point of view. We do, however, yearn to place our experiences of art within the contexts of our lives, our larger worlds, and here we can say that whatever their sources in the personal histories and genetics of their composers, the musics of Webern and Feldman (and countless others from recent years) make possible for us a relationship to silence, and the room it gives us, that would seem otherwise impossible in a deafening age. The properties in their musics that accomplish this are not unique to them, of course, any more than the perception that the world is getting louder is unique to us as moderns. These are both matters of degree. It is probable that in two hundred years—if we are still in a position to have this kind of discussion—the level and din of information exchange— aural,digital, and (who knows) psychic— may make our current age seem as a veritable Walden. That doesn't mean we don't have a problem.

For us to be able to enter the world that music creates for us, we need a silence within which to listen. It will be said in response that in many cultures music is not presented as an object of veneration within a temple of adoring quietude, but rather as part of the rush and tumult of everyday life; thus we should not need the expectant hush of the concert hall ourselves (and just who are "we," anyway?). These are valid points, and do challenge the clear subject/object separation that classical music culture, at least, has tended to enforce. In most world societies, however, there are spaces, even if only interior, set aside for contemplation, for noiseless recalibration of the soul, and in ours there are almost none. Our places of worship, by and large, have given themselves over to a muzak-based sense of liturgy. New-age bookstores, with their palmists and meditation rooms, surround their patrons with a noxious haze of synthesizers, pennywhistles and Inuit drums; like dairy cattle, customers become more productive if encouraged in their purchases by this kind of marginal musical discourse. That the message to buy here takes the form of a willfully soporific cassation of juvenile spiritual pretensions makes it that much more noxious, for what primary experience are we having here? Are we listeners seeking an archetype of beauty, or seekers listening for the godhead? It turns out we are neither—though we may have been duped into one or the other conviction. We are consumers.

This practice is not limited to the "metaphysical" book industry, of course. If we frequent any number of the hipper clothing chains we will find ourselves buoyed by rave or trip-hop jams that serve to wash away the sense of complicity we feel in supporting a sweatshop economy; the music is telling us that we belong here, that we're different, were aware, we're not the problem. We're down with the Homies, with the Latinos, with the fags and dikes, with the left and the right. We're down with EVERYONE; we don't want any trouble, we just want to buy a pair of cargo pants. Once again, the absence of silence makes it impossible for us to decode the onslaught before we've succumbed to it. And this is not just a function of capitalism. It's worse.

We find ourselves as a culture unable to assuage our loneliness except through the ceaseless accompaniment of our everyday actions. In such a world buying a book or a shirt is not merely to acquire a thing, to fill a need; it is, rather, to participate in the forced scripting of our lives according to commercial fabuli that tell us, through the soundtrack by which we buy, eat, make love, crap, worship and, eventually, die, not who we are but who we wish we were. Even our sense of time becomes hopelessly distorted, as we float through our lives according to the dreamlike spans of musical phrases rather than the waking rhythms of clock-time. Thus our capacity to be present for our lives, for our work especially, is compromised by a time-sense that is artificially constructed along unconscious models in order to give perspective on the conscious experience of time's passing. In losing silence, and the corresponding potential for musical discernment that silence engenders, we lose ourselves.

This, perhaps, is what Ligeti had in mind in the fourth movement of his *Piano Concerto*, where silence eventually succombs to madness. As in all of Ligeti's music, spaces in the work, both textural and temporal, are gradually filled in through a dizzied layering of canon and pitch-cycle. In most of his recent works, however, there is always space through which to "view" the process; the greatest premium is placed on clarity of both gesture and phrase trajectory (such is the case with the other four movements of the *Concerto*). In the fourth movement of this work, however, early silences of anywhere from six to eight beats are gradually compressed, until by the movement's climax silence has been obliterated through an orchestral canon of nine parts, which eventually spins itself into nothingness. Ligeti provides no program, but the effect is that of any number of daily contemporary situations wherein sound is deafening but sense is absent.

Sense may seem to return, of course, the moment we strap into our Discmen. The "personal stereo" as it's called makes available to us conditions that are near-anechoic. Crowned with headphones we plunge into a total aural void, within which the silences of Webern, Feldman, Ligeti, Haydn, Ravi Shankar or a templeful of Tibetan monks become real and rich for us once again. This would seem the ultimate solution to our problem, the most perfect means of apprehending music's symbiosis with silence, until we consider two discomfiting realities: in voluntarily wearing headphones we are agreeing to the taming, by actual, physical sound, of our own interior landscapes (a last frontier, one could say), and we agree to go the process alone, for no one can reach us when we are plugged-in in this way. In this state we become slaves to a jealous god who seeks to rob us of our deepest capacities for expression and relationship. For the silences of Webern, of Feldman, Haydn, Beethoven, Miles Davis and (yes!) Jimi Hendrix were conceived of as shared fields of sonic space. It is only now that they are being parcelled off and sold, one by one, to individual buyers. The unanimous hush that fell with Hendrix' final, plaintive, nightmarish phrases in the live new year's eve 1970 recording of *Machine Gun*, has now receded into the akasha; the sense of wonder it inspired has long since been replaced with a knowing sense of style, an aesthetic shorthand of narrowing signification. This is fundamental to the transformation of any art, of course, and is not necessarily a terrible thing. What is pernicious here, pernicious simply because of the ease and semi-conscious assent with which it is happening, is that the common sense of "Oh my God" that greets the best work of any artist is now more likely to occur as a singular, individual event, outside the frame of any human relationship. The hush that Hendrix inspired, the result of genuine stylistic, technical and expressive transcendence acted out in the real presence of an engaged community, has little or no counterpart in today's media culture.

Thus is the communal experience, the sharing, of music made a solitary enterprise; thus is the antidote for the poison of unwanted sound made an instrument of isolation and estrangement; thus are thoughts which once sounded only in the imagination drenched in a shower of overtones; thus is music rendered impotent to the point of non-existence; thus is the colonization of silence complete.

What then to do? Are we left simply to handwringing and despair? Do we lash out at a basic aspect of modern life which, in the end, none of us can help but enable? Do we smash loudspeakers, hurl our neighbor's Discman to the ground? Probably not. No luddite sensibility can survive this age; we've come too far, too fast. Even as I write this angry missive I, like every other musician I know, am striving to hear through the noise and find what is essential in it, what speaks uniquely of my and my neighborhood's experience and to sing of that in my music. To hate the media is to hate ourselves: we all want the big medicine in the magic box to touch us, to dazzle us, to heal us. We know that ultimately it can't, but we simply don't know how or where to stop, we're children eating skittles; our mouths are full and we just want more. To pretend otherwise is, I think, poignant at best.

There are certainly things we can do in our own lives, however, in our own relationships to sound, to conserve sonic spaces and find again the grace that silence bestows, to find room to hear again, without destroying property or attacking each other. Three in particular come to mind. You can take or leave them; I offer them here:

Don't listen to music; listen to the world, and learn to distinguish between the two. Music can exist for you then.

Don't shop in malls.

Find silent places and then.........be quiet.

ROBERT ASHLEY is one of the prominent avant garde composers for the theater. His work has influenced such composers as Phillip Glass, Meredith Monk, and Laurie Anderson. Among his renowned operas are, *Perfect Lives, Improvement, El Aficionado*, and *Dust*. "When the 21st Century glances back to see where the future of opera came from—The Village Voice comments—Ashley, like Monteverdi before him, is going to look like a radical new beginning."

TRISHA BROWN is one of America's foremost choreographers. Since 1979, she has been working in large-scale theatrical collaborations with prominent artists from the visual arts and music fields. Her works have been performed all over the world. Her latest major piece was *El Trilogy*, a three-part, 90-minute show, performed in July 2001 at The Lincoln Center Festival, in New York City.

PEDRO CUPERMAN teaches Latin American Literature and Semiotics at Syracuse University. Among his works are *Tango*, coauthored with Nancy Graves, and *Go East by Going West*, coauthored with Izhar Patkin. His book *Diario de Viaje* was released by Scholastic in 1996 and subsequently adopted by the School Board of the State of California.

ELKA KRAJEWSKA born in Poland, is an artist living in New York. Her digital micro-movies have been exhibited at various group shows in New York City, most recently at Exit Art and Paul Rodgers.

MARCO MAGGI born in Uruguay, is an artist living in New York. His work has been exhibited in galleries and museums in the USA and Europe. His most recent show was in San Francisco at the Hosfeld Gallery. Presently he is exhibiting at the Mercosur Bienal in Brazil.

JEFFREY MEHLMAN is a University Professor at Boston University and author, most recently, of *Émigré New York: French Intellectuals in Wartime Manhattan, Genealogies of the Text,* and *Walter Benjamin for Children: An Essay on His Radio Years.*

PANAYIOTIS MICHAEL was born and lives in Cyprus and studied art in Moscow and New York City. Since 1994 his work has been exhibited in personal and group shows in the USA and Europe, most recently in Germany at the Siemens Kultur Programm.

NAM JUNE PAIK "I make technology ridiculous," he says in the first image of his website. He is known as the father of video art and influences the younger generation of artists. Nam June Paik was kind enough to design the front and back covers of this special issue of *Point of Contact* on Silence.

RAIMON PANIKKAR is a renown philosopher and theologian. Among his many books are *Invisible Harmony, Cosmotheandric Experience*, and *Unknown Pilgrims*. He lives in Tavertet (Catalunya), Spain, and regularly lectures around the world and in India.

IZHAR PATKIN is an Israeli-born artist who lives and works in New York City. Among his works are *The Black Paintings*, 1985-86 (The Museum of Modern Art, NY); *Don Quijote Segunda Parte*, 1987 (The Guggenheim Museum, NY); *Where Each Is Both*, 1994 (The Guggenheim Museum, NY).

OWEN SHAPIRO is an independent and experimental filmmaker. He directs the Film Program at Syracuse University. Among his films are *Thomas Szasz and The Myth of Mental Illness, and Many Happy Returns*, which won first prize at the Athens International Film Festival and first prize at the Jewish Video Film Festival in Berkley, California.

ANA TISCORNIA is a Uruguayan artist who lives in Tribeca, New York City. Her work has been exhibited nationally and internationally. At the present time she is part of the exhibition *Politicas de la diferencia* (Politics of Difference), a traveling exhibition on Latin American artists.

ANDREW WAGGONER is a composer and past director of the School of Music at Syracuse University. Several of his compositions have been recorded, including *Train and A Song . . . (Strophic Variations For String Quartet.)*

PETER WOLLEN wrote, among other books, *Signs and Meanings in the Cinema* and *Raiding the Icebox: Reflections on Twentieth-Century Culture*. Among his films are *Riddles of the Sphinx*, made in collaboration with Laura Mulvey. He also coauthored the script of Michelangelo Antonioni's *The Passenger*. He teaches film at the University of California, Los Angeles.

POINT OF CONTACT

Subscribe Today

- ❑ $25 individual issues
- ❑ $45 - 1 yr individual subscription (2 issues)
- ❑ $75 - 1 yr institution subscription (2 issues)
- ❑ $30 back issues
- ❑ $ Donation ______________________

Please make checks payable to:
Point of Contact
Syracuse University
216 H. B. Crouse Hall
Syracuse, New York 13244-1160

Name ______________________________

Address __________________ City _______

State __________________ Zip _______

Amount Enclosed ______________________

POINT OF CONTACT

A PARTIAL LIST OF PAST TEXTS

1975 Vol. 1, No. 1
Jean Franco, "The Limits of the Liberal Imagination: *One Hundred Years of Solitude* and *Nostromo*"; Raimundo Panikkar, "The Message of Yesterday's India to Today's World." Also texts by Pedro Cuperman, Noe Jitrik, Jose Ruibal, and Jacqueline Simon. Poetry: Christopher Middleton. Art: Abdias Do Nascimento.

1976 Vol. 1, No. 2
Dina Sherzer and Joel Sherzer, "A Semiotic Analysis of Cuna Molas"; Beaujour, Hoffa, Wilhelm, "Periplum on Pound at Syracuse University.

Vol. 1, No. 3
Warren Dean, "The USIA Book Program: How translations of 'politically correct' books are secretly subsidized for sale in Latin Amercia," Nicolas Calas, "Jasper Johns and the critique of painting"

1977 Vol. 1, No. 4
W. D. Snodgrass, "Four Spanish Songs"; Guadalupe Valdes Faffis, "Sociolinguistics of Chicano Literature,"

1978 Vol. 2, No. 1
Julio Cortázar, "Cinco Sonetos Eróticos"; Raimundo Panikkar, "The Texture of a Text: In Response to P. Ricoeur"; Manuel Puig, "Pubis Angelical (fragment)."

1979 Vol. 2, No. 2
Bernadette Bucher, "Words into Images: Semiotics of Text Illustration"; Carlos Fuentes, "The Writer in an Alien Culture"; Mercedes Lopez-Baralt, "Millenarism as liminality: the Andean myth of Ikarri."

1981 Vol. 2, #3/4
P.E.N. Conference on Desaparecidos and Tortured In Latin America: Texts by Jaime Alazraki, Dore Ashton, Andrés Avellaneda, Jorge Lima Barreto, Ramsey Clark, Pablo Antonio Cuadra, Pedro Cuperman, Peter Falk, Isaac Goldemberg, Oscar Hahn, Luis Harss, Severo Sarduy, Carlos Martinez Moreno, Luisa Valenzuela, and Saúl Yurkievich. Art by: Juan Acha, Denise Green, and Teodoro Maus.

1982 Vol. 3, No. 1/2
Jacques Garelli, "Sartre and the Question of the Subject"; Severo Sarduy, 'Barroco de la Substraccion"; Hector Libertella, 'Octavio Paz: El Text Portagrama o Lider."

1993 Vol. 3, No. 3
The Americas Baroque: Texts by Rolando Hinojosa-Smith, Elena Poniatowska, José Sanjinés, Severo Sarduy, Douglas Unger, Saúl Yurkievich, Pedro Cuperman and Peter Wollen. Art by Marta Chilindron, Eduardo Costa, Nancy Graves, Kristina Colovic, Izhar Patkin, Nam June Paik, Joseph Kugielsky, Rimma Gerlovina, Valeriy Gerlovin, and William Wegman.

1994 Vol. 4, No. 1
Julio Cortázar 1914-1984: Texts by Julio Cortázar, Jean Andreu, Julio Ortega, Saúl Yurkievich, Jaime Alazraki, José Sanjinés, Alicia Borinsky, Carlos A. Rabasso, and Pedro Cuperman. Art by Caspi, Liliana Porter, Julio Silva, Joseph Kugielsky, and Ursula Von Rydingsvard.

1995 Vol. 4, No. 2
Writing Across Cultures: Texts by Douglas Unger, Bob Shacochis, Ana Castillo, Irene Vilar, Osvaldo Sabino, Christopher Leland, David William Foster and Pedro Cuperman. Art by Nancy Graves, Ana Tiscomia, Jaime Davidovich, Hung Liu, Jane Hammond.

1997 Vol. 5, #1
Eye On Cinema: Conversations with Haile Gerima, Phillip Glass, Amy Tan, Wayne Wang. Texts by Pedro Cuperman, Gloria J. Gibson, Owen Shapiro, Andrew Waggoner, Peter Wollen, and John Yau. Art by: Papo Colo, Gregory Crewdson, Rob Van Erve, Joseph Kugielsky, Sean Landers, Judy Pfaff, and Sandy Skoglund.

INTRODUCING........

POINT OF CONTACT PRODUCTIONS...

a division of Punto de Contacto/ Point of Contact Inc.

Presents...

POETRY...

Corresponding Voices Vol. I (November 2001)
A volume of poetry by Michael Jennings, Edgar Paiewonsky-Conde, Kerry Shawn Keys, Suzanne Shane, and Lila Zemborain.
Cover designed by Liliana Porter

Corresponding Voices is the first in a series of poetry books to be published by Point of Contact Productions.

And...

ORIGINAL ART...

The *MacIntosh Apples*, hand carved by Uruguayan-born artist Marco Maggi, are the first in a series of limited edition art offered exclusively through *Point of Contact* by the generous support of the artists.

Maggi carves what could be described as scriptural circuitry in apples. His creations and the ideas behind them were part of a recent *Art News* article (April 2001) on the phenomenon of micro art. Each apple (limited to an edition of 50 apples only) can be purchased for $300 ($200 being a donation to Punto de Contacto/Point of Contact, Inc. a non-profit organization).

For details or purchasing, please write or call:
Christina Fawcett at Point of Contact
Syracuse University, 216 H.B. Crouse Bldg.
Syr., NY 13224-1160 phone 315-443-2247